PRAISE

Preaching Punchlines

"*I think Jerry Seinfeld should invite Susan Sparks to be a guest on* Comedians in Cars Getting Coffee. . . . *But this book is the next best thing . . . an irresistible new lens for looking at the world, and your preaching.*"

—ANNA CARTER FLORENCE
PETER MARSHALL PROFESSOR OF PREACHING, COLUMBIA THEOLOGICAL SEMINARY

"*Susan Sparks is a spiritual musician and sacred chef capable of composing whimsical, ironic, and powerful spiritual truths . . . Do yourself a favor and 'taste and see' what this literary chef has prepared for your hungry soul.*"

—OTIS MOSS III
SENIOR PASTOR, TRINITY UNITED CHURCH OF CHRIST, CHICAGO, ILLINOIS

"*Susan has beautifully distilled exactly how to bring more humor, warmth, joy, and impact to our sermons. Bonus: This is the most fun book on preaching you'll ever read!*"

—THE REV. PETER M. WALLACE
PRODUCER & HOST, 'DAY1'
AUTHOR OF *THE PASSIONATE JESUS* AND *HEART AND SOUL*

"Preaching Punchlines *provides playful and practical exercises to enliven our sermons and thus finally awaken those in the pews.*"

—JONATHAN L. WALTON
PLUMMER PROFESSOR OF CHRISTIAN MORALS (FAS)
PUSEY MINISTER TO THE MEMORIAL CHURCH
PROFESSOR OF RELIGION AND SOCIETY (HDS)

Susan Sparks is a beloved preacher and nationally known speaker thanks to her skill wrapping wisdom in humor. In her newest book, *Preaching Punchlines*, Susan—well—preaches what she practices!

—Rabbi Bob Alper
Comedian and author

It should be obvious that the Rev. Susan Sparks has a great sense of humor when she is asking me, a Jew, to write a few words about her new book where she tries to teach preachers how to infuse their sermons with comedy. In lovely, sweet, and humorous lessons, she has done a wonderful job that is simple, direct, and to the point. She has given a road map to helping find one's sense of humor and how to use it. From preachers to public speakers, it's a book you're going to want to read and refer to. With what I've learned, I just may show up preaching at a church near you.

—Lewis Black
Comedian

Susan Sparks is a refreshing voice of hope in a time of doubt and of humor in a time of angst. While not denying the shadowy sides of life, her bright and bold perspective consistently helps us locate the Light. A don't-miss read for preachers . . . and everybody else who needs a faith lift!

—Dr. Michael B. Brown
Speaker, minister, author, professor
Former senior minister, Marble Collegiate Church, New York City

Reading *Preaching Punchlines* is like sitting down with Susan Sparks over a tall glass of sweet tea and having a good laugh. You leave refreshed and a bit tired from the laughter but, nonetheless, inspired. Describing humor as one of the most powerful rhetorical tools available, Sparks shows how a preacher (or any communicator) can use humor to communicate the life-giving messages of God because "humor is nothing but a learned skill." *Preaching Punchlines* is filled with practical statistics ("studies show that an audience will form a judgment of a speaker or performer in approximately ten seconds"), tips ("if you find yourself conjugating more than seven Hebrew verbs in a sermon, you've lost your audience") and facts ("medical studies prove the connection between humor and memory"). The book is peppered with QR codes that take you off across many disciplines to prove points and offer suggestions. This trial lawyer turned comedian and Baptist preacher is doing her part to ensure more inspiring sermons in pulpits everywhere.

—*Linda Post Bushkofsky*
Executive Director, Women of the ELCA

Preaching Punchlines: The Ten Commandments of Comedy is Susan Sparks at her best in blending grace-filled faith and laughter. She reminds us that worship should be and can be a joyful experience. *Preaching Punchlines* is packed full of practical advice and words of wisdom about using humor to connect with congregations, embracing creativity in preaching, and framing sermons so that people will listen, remember, and share.

—*Pam Durso*
Executive director, Baptist Women in Ministry
Atlanta, Georgia

I think Jerry Seinfeld should invite Susan Sparks to be a guest on *Comedians in Cars Getting Coffee,* so they can talk about what preachers and comedians have in common while riding a Harley down the Long Island Expressway. But this book is the next best thing. It's hilarious, it's astute, it's profound, and it has practical tools that really work. It will also give you an irresistible new lens for looking at the world, and your preaching.

—*Anna Carter Florence*
Peter Marshall Professor of Preaching
Columbia Theological Seminary

A preacher with a motorcycle, cowboy boots, a wicked sense of humor, and a heart that warms you like a huge Southern-style breakfast. That's my pastor!

—*Tamron Hall*
Broadcast journalist and television host

Too often as preachers we are overwhelmed by the cacophony of bad news and sad stories in the world. We seem to have forgotten the joy inherent in the "good news"—the hope inherent in God's laughter. Susan Sparks draws on her amazing gifts as a preacher, stand-up comic, and trial lawyer not only to guide us back into the flow of the divine comedy but also to use its power to heal and inspire our congregations and our world.

—*Rev. Dr. J. Peter Holmes*
Minister of the Congregation
Yorkminster Park Baptist Church, Toronto, Canada

In *Preaching Punchlines*, the Reverend Susan Sparks reminds us that while the Gospel story should be taken seriously, we Christians might do well not to take ourselves too seriously trying to live it. In this fine volume, she helps us find our way to laughter and to grace.

—*Bill J. Leonard*
Dunn Professor of Baptist Studies and Church History Emeritus
Wake Forest University

Often we pick up a book, examine the cover, and wonder "will this book speak to me?" If you are reading this blurb the "Spirit" is calling you to read this book! Susan Sparks is a spiritual musician and sacred chef capable of composing whimsical, ironic, and powerful spiritual truths with pen, paper, and observant wit. I have witnessed her gift—in person and upon the pages of the book you now hold—crack open the hardened parts of the human soul and offer grace, a culinary delicacy we all desire but many are afraid to taste. Do yourself a favor and "taste and see" what this literary chef has prepared for your hungry soul.

—*Otis Moss III*
Senior Pastor, Trinity United Church of Christ
Chicago, Illinois

Susan Sparks is deeply funny. Her book is an invaluable guide to pastors who want to bring joy and laughter along with spirituality to their congregations.

—*Stephen Rosenfield*
Director, American Comedy Institute

Religion is too important to leave in the hands of the joyless. In *Preaching Punchlines*, pastor and stand-up comedian Susan Sparks teaches us to use laughter to shatter our defenses and open our hearts. This is a book for anyone who knows that laughter and love work best when they work together.

—*Rabbi Rami Shapiro*
Author of *Holy Rascals*
Co-author of the Mount and Mountain series and
Beginnings: A Reverend and a Rabbi Talk about the Stories of Genesis

Effectively using humor as she speaks truth to power in an effort to change people and shake them from their stagnation, the wit, wisdom, and intelligence of Rev. Susan Sparks shines through wherever she goes, whatever the venue. *Preaching Punchlines* is for anyone who appreciates the deft use of humor with just the right words delivered in just the right ways . . . not only from the pulpit, but on stage, in corporate board rooms, or in a variety of other public speaking situations. By any standard, *Preaching Punchlines* is an outstanding humor handbook for all of us.

—*Edward J. Trayes*
Professor of Journalism, Temple University

The amazing Susan Sparks has come down from the mountaintop carrying two stone tablets with ten comedy commandments just for preachers (there were 15, but unfortunately she dropped a tablet). Susan has beautifully distilled exactly how to bring more humor, warmth, joy, and impact to our sermons. Bonus: This is the most fun book on preaching you'll ever read!

—*The Rev. Peter M. Wallace*
Producer & host, "Day1," and author of
The Passionate Jesus and *Heart and Soul*

It's no secret that a cross-section of American society regards stand-up comedians as the prophets of our day. A comedian's capacity to speak truth to power, hold up a mirror of self-criticism, and make us laugh at the absurd is their true gift. As both comedian and preacher, Susan Sparks is neither ready to cede the centrality of the Gospel nor accept the conventional, dull

Sunday morning pulpit sedative. *Preaching Punchlines* provides playful and practical exercises to enliven our sermons and thus finally awaken those in the pews.

—*Jonathan L. Walton*
Plummer Professor of Christian Morals (FAS)
Pusey Minister to the Memorial Church
Professor of Religion and Society (Harvard Divinity School)

How many preachers ever think, "My congregation deserves joy"? But that's the key question that Susan Sparks puts to us in this lively, practical, and searching book, which will make seasoned (i.e., jaded) preachers think again and look at what is demanded of them in what ought to be the joyful role of communicating the divine comedy of healing and transfiguration.

—*Rowan (not Atkinson, alas) Williams*
Former Archbishop of Canterbury

PREACHING PUNCHLINES

Also by Susan Sparks

Laugh Your Way to Grace

Smyth & Helwys Publishing, Inc.
6316 Peake Road
Macon, Georgia 31210-3960
1-800-747-3016
©2019 by Susan Sparks
All rights reserved.

Library of Congress Cataloging-in-Publication Data

Names: Sparks, Susan, 1962- author.
Title: Preaching punchlines : the ten commandments of comedy / by
  Susan Sparks.
Description: Macon : Smyth & Helwys, 2019. | Includes bibliographical
  references.
Identifiers: LCCN 2019008884 | ISBN 9781641731386 (pbk. : alk. paper)
Subjects: LCSH: Preaching. | Wit and humor--Religious aspects--Christianity.
Classification: LCC BV4235.H85 S63 2019 | DDC 251--dc23
LC record available at https://lccn.loc.gov/2019008884

Preaching Punchlines

THE TEN COMMANDMENTS OF COMEDY

SUSAN SPARKS

To my beloved husband, Toby, who makes me laugh
more than anyone on the face of this earth.
And to my wee granddaughter, Madeleine, and my great-nephew, Reed,
the newest members of our family,
who remind us—every day—that our sense of joy is still there.

ACKNOWLEDGMENTS

Huge thanks to my congregational family at Madison Avenue Baptist Church, who have for years blessed me with the gifts of patience, time, and a wide berth to develop as a preacher and a comedian.

To my publisher Smyth & Helwys, my editor Leslie Andres, cover designers Daniel Emerson and Brace Thomson, who all believed in this book and worked so diligently for its publication.

For the great humor theologian warriors who blazed the trail before me, including among others Conrad Hyers, Harvey Cox, Doug Adams, Fred Craddock, Elton Trueblood, and Joseph Webb.

For the owner of that boot shop in far west Texas who, in January 2000, convinced me that the confidence I needed to follow my call as a comedian and a preacher could be found in a great pair of Tony Lamas.

Most of all, heartfelt thanks to my friends and family, who have accompanied me from courtrooms to pulpits to dark, smoky comedy clubs. Despite me being me, you have shared nothing but love and appreciation. For that, I am eternally grateful.

Contents

Introduction

Religion has actually convinced people that there's an invisible man—living in the sky—who watches everything you do, every minute of every day. And the invisible man has a special list of ten things he does not want you to do. And if you do any of these ten things, he has a special place, full of fire and smoke and burning and torture and anguish, where he will send you to live and suffer and burn and choke and scream and cry forever and ever 'til the end of time. But He loves you . . . and He needs money.

—George Carlin, *Politically Incorrect*, May 29, 1997

I'm a big believer in getting to the point. So let me share the bottom line of this book up front: smart, focused, joyful communication is a matter of life and death—especially in preaching. I offer the Apostle Paul as proof:

> And upon the first day of the week, when the disciples came together to break bread, Paul preached unto them, ready to depart on the morrow; and *continued his speech until midnight.* And there were many lights in the upper chamber, where they were gathered together. And there sat in a window a certain young man named Eutychus, being fallen into a deep sleep: and as Paul was *long preaching*, he [Eutychus] sunk down with sleep, and fell down from the third loft, and was taken up dead. (Acts 20:7-9, KJV, italics mine)

This book will teach you how to avoid killing people. OK, so maybe your congregation or audience won't drop out of a window, but words can still kill in other sinister ways. They can slay people's spirits, eradicate their joy, gut their passion. Words can alienate, divide, shame, and destroy community. They can corrode budding spiritual seekers through boredom, irrelevance, or confusion.

I write this book not only as a preacher and a comedian but also as a ten-year trial lawyer, a debate coach, a workshop leader, an author, a nationally syndicated columnist, a corporate trainer in executive presentation skills, a TEDx speaker, and, clearly, someone suffering from multiple personality disorder.

My point? Don't put this book down just because you don't step into a pulpit every week or you aren't religious. It is titled *Preaching Punchlines* because, frankly, my preacher peeps and I need humor the most. But the lessons in this book are relevant for anyone who communicates for a living. All y'all (a Southern phrase meaning everyone) are invited to the party.

Why am I writing it? I believe that ministers and stand-up comedians have the same job. We both are called to stand in solidarity with people during the crazy, annoying times of life and the times of tragedy. When done right, the work of both ministers and comedians makes people feel a little less alone. When our work is done wrong, we can cut people to the core. Sadly, I spent years estranged from the church because of the latter.

My early memory of worship was walking in, bracing myself for the body blow of shame, then walking out bent over and beaten down three inches shorter. Now, as an ordained minister and a stand-up comedian, I feel called to say, "Enough!" There is a time to weep and a time to laugh—and we have erred way too hard on the side of weeping.

Our places of worship have gotten too caught up in self-importance and solemnity, the idea that we have to be serious *in* church to be serious *about* church. Why can't we encourage people to laugh in church? We are made in the image of the divine, and *we* laugh; therefore a part of the divine must also encompass joy and laughter.

Always lurking in the wings are the skeptics who believe humor is not appropriate in holy realms. Let me take thirty seconds right now to debunk the top four arguments against using humor in a pulpit:

1. It's blasphemous. To whom? God? As if God doesn't appreciate a little levity? It's like Voltaire said: "God is a comedian playing to an audience who's afraid to laugh." Perhaps pride is the more blasphemous threat.

2. Humor is the newest tool in a line of cute, trendy ways to build a mega-church. Ah, not exactly. The first example of humor in religion was in the fifteenth century BCE in the Mesopotamian Myth of Adapa, and for thousands of years since then, almost every major world religious tradition has honored its power. Christianity—not so much.[1]

3. Humor has no place in serious theology. Aristotle, Plato, Kant, Kierkegaard, Nietzsche, Hobbes, Bergeson, Freud, and Reinhold Niebuhr disagree.

4. Humor can be dangerous. When I say "humor," I am referring to joyful, therapeutic humor, humor that lifts us up, humor that honors. I am not speaking of scornful, rude, hateful, or judgmental humor. Certainly, humor can be misused. So can sanctity.

I rest my case.

Humor, laughter, and comedy should organically ooze out of the Christian tradition. It is no coincidence that the Greek word for gospel is *euaggelion.* With my Southern accent, that comes out something like "you-ah-jellyin." While on its face it may sound like an item that you slather on toast, the literal translation of the word is "good news."

Good news.

---

1. If you are interested in an analysis of humor in ancient and modern Christian practices as well as in world religious traditions, scan here where you'll find a complimentary copy of my honors thesis at Union Theological Seminary, "Laughing Your Way to Grace: A Study in Humor and the Sacred."

Hmm. Not hearing that much on Sundays. So again, where's the joy?

The sad fact is that church numbers are plummeting while the number of spiritual seekers is staying stable if not increasing. People are hungry for spiritual food. And we have food—lots of it! The problem ain't the food. It's how we're serving it. Kind of like okra. Stewed, it's nasty and slimy and no one wants it. But fried, it's a gift from heaven. We're stewin' the good news, if you get my drift.

To remedy this, I have created what I call the "Ten Commandments of Comedy" to demonstrate how tools from stand-up comedy can transform our preaching and help us better honor this message of "good news." Each chapter addresses a commandment or collection of lessons that I've learned as a professional comedian and explains its practical application to a pulpit. I've also included an appendix with sermons and sample material, as well as QR codes throughout the text that you can scan with your smartphone to access additional information and videos.

To be clear, this book is not a

- compilation of sermon jokes;
- training manual for how to be funny at the beginning of the sermon; or
- primer on how to become a professional stand-up comedian. (If that is what you want, buy *Mastering Stand-up* by Stephen Rosenfield, my comedy coach. Then close this book and go with God.)

This book *is* about
- generating intimacy and honesty in worship;
- framing messages that people will listen to, remember, and share;
- finding your creative voice;
- forming instant trust and rapport with your congregation or audience;
- building bridges and defusing conflict; and
- sharing the fullest, most authentic version of yourself in the pulpit, which includes your sense of joy. (Even if you don't realize it's still there. It is.)

In the end, we are bringing together two things—humor and religion—that, while seeming unrelated, desperately need each other.

So join me! Take a risk and tap your creativity. Step into the pulpit with joy and confidence and see what great things are possible.

Chapter 1

Thou Shalt Remember Thou Art Creative

If you have made people laugh, you are a comedy writer. Sometimes people who haven't written comedy before think of comedy writers as wizards, possessed of magical powers inaccessible to mere mortals. . . . comedy writing is work— nothing more, nothing less. And the harder you work at it, the better you get. . . . think of "comedy writer" as a hat, and put it on your head and keep it there.

—Stephen Rosenfield, founder, American Comedy Institute
and author of *Mastering Stand-up: The Complete Guide to
Becoming a Successful Comedian*

The question I get more than any other—more than "What's the meaning of life?", or "Why do people suffer?", or "Why are the New England Patriots so . . . them?"—is "Can I learn to be funny?" Pastors love to throw out every imaginable caveat when they hear that I teach comedy to preachers: "Oh, I'm not really that funny." "I don't think I have much of a talent for comedy." Or my personal favorite, "Don't expect much."

Well, brothers and sisters, let me pull back the curtain in front of the great Oz: humor is nothing but a learned skill. Ta-da. That's it. (Sorry to disappoint those of you who thought you had the ironclad excuse. You don't.) You put in the work, and you can do it. It is absolutely possible. And you start with yourself.

Work on Thyself

If you hear a voice within you saying, "You are not a painter," then by all means paint, boy, and that voice will be silenced.

—Vincent Van Gogh

There is one place where comedy and preaching totally and utterly diverge: the world of being surly. Surly works in comedy. Serious, somber, morose, or depressed works in comedy. It-does-not-work-in-the-church. (By the way, hyphens are a trick to emphasize words in comedy.)

People come to houses of worship not necessarily to laugh but to find comfort, to be lifted up. If the preacher's expressions and mannerisms do nothing but mirror the pain in the pews, why would anyone ever return? Even Jesus' most heartfelt words fall flat if uttered from a flat heart.

I said earlier that comedy is a learned skill, but I *should* say it's a remembered skill. We had it at birth. According to studies, kids laugh approximately 400 times a day while adults laugh about 20 times per day. I'm pretty sure that's why Jesus said we must become like the little children. They laugh more. They smile more. They don't carry the weight of the world on their faces (unless they're hungry or sitting in poop, which are legitimate reasons to scowl).

My comedy partner, Rabbi Bob Alper, shares a story in his act from the 1950s program *The Art Linkletter Show*. In it, a little boy tells Linkletter that his dog died. Linkletter says, "It's OK, I'm sure your dog is in heaven." The little boy then scrunches up his face and says, "What would God want with a dead dog?!"

Kids have an innate, yet fresh sense of creativity. When we were young, we were naturally creative, using the entire box of Crayola crayons to invent wondrous, colorful stick people, animals, and floating clouds. And why not? We are all children of an artistic genius. Take thirty seconds and gaze on these National Geographic photos of creation and tell me I'm wrong.

I've always believed that we most resemble God at the time we were handed out of God's arms to our parents. This includes being honest, playful, and quick to laugh. But something happens between birth and, as some people refer to it, "maturity" (although I tend to think that kids are more grounded than us "mature" adults). Whatever you call the aging process, the fact is that over time the world closes in. Our shoulders droop under the weight of our lives. Our sense of joy gets squeezed out. And we slowly begin to believe all the chatter that says we should act a certain way, we should live a certain way, and, worst of all, we don't deserve joy.

Jesus taught that "whatever you ask for in prayer, believe that you have received it, and it will be yours" (Mark 11:24). You have to believe it to receive it. Before you take any steps toward studying comedy as a preacher, you have to believe that your own heart is worthy to receive joy.

Looking for the Funny

The most regretful people on earth are those who felt the call to creative work, who felt their own creative power restive and uprising, and gave to it neither power nor time.

—Mary Oliver, poet

One of the greatest maladies in the clergy world (and frankly, the world at large) is that we have forgotten we can laugh. The world does its best to beat the joy out of us. But here's the good news: it's still there. We just have to find it. Every human being, no matter how crusty or cantankerous, has something that will make him or her laugh. Some people watch *Saturday Night Live*. Others read the works of David Sedaris. Still others binge on YouTube videos about cats. Whatever floats your boat. The point is that somewhere in this great big world, there is something that will make you laugh. Find it—and remember you can laugh. Once you do that, you've officially started your training in the craft of comedy.

A comedian learns to see the world through the lens of humor. Similarly, people who want to inject humor in their sermons or lectures need to train their eyes to see it and their ears to hear it. For example, musicians train their ears by listening to music. Chefs train their palates by tasting. Comedians learn by watching comedy.

These days there is no excuse. There are televisions, computers, iPads, iPhones, YouTube, podcasts, SiriusXM radio. Identify people who make you laugh. Adopt them as your virtual comedy coaches. Study what they do, how they do it, their topics, their delivery. Slowly, it will begin to sink in. You'll start to notice comic things. You'll laugh more. You'll start to look for the funny.

It's like buying a new car. For example, you purchase a red Toyota Highlander. After you drive it home, for the next few days, weeks, or even months, you start seeing all these red Highlanders on the road! Why are all these people buying *my car*? Then you realize that by purchasing one, you have attuned yourself to seeing red Highlanders.

It's the same with comedy and humor. You can attune yourself to noticing funny things when it becomes a part of your life—when you "own" it. Then you are on your way to forming your own unique voice and perspective.

Shake It Up

A comfort zone is a beautiful place, but nothing ever grows there.

—John Assaraf

People talk a lot about writer's block: the inability to access our creativity. That stuff's for real. Anyone who writes for a living, especially preachers who write sermons every single week, knows about its ugly claws. Sometimes it's caused by self-doubt, other times exhaustion or emotional flatness. Whatever the reason, the only solution I've found to break the cycle is based on gardening.

To me, the creative process is like rescuing a root-bound potted plant. At some point, the pot becomes too small, the roots bind up and are unable to absorb nutrients, and the plant starts to wilt and die. To bring it back to life, you take it out of its pot, shake the roots free, replant it in a bigger pot with fresh dirt and fertilizer, and watch it begin to flourish again.

Our comedy voice and preaching voice are the same as that plant. Over the years, the world wears us down. We become insular, jaded, burned out. Our world gets small. Our ability to absorb nutrients, to see creatively, to think in new and innovative ways, to experience or, God forbid, share joy is squeezed out of us, like living in a pot that is five times too small for us. In order to bring that creative voice back—to remember it—we must shake it up. One way to do that is by changing our perspective.

Part of my ordination process was a requirement that all candidates undergo two days of psychological testing. There were the standard questions and interviews. But then there was the Rorschach ink dot test. If you've never taken the test, suffice it to say it is a lesson in creativity. The interviewer showed me a piece of paper with ink dots splattered on it—a bit reminiscent of Jackson Pollock. I, as the interviewee, was to tell him what I saw. Then again, I knew this was a screening test for ordination. So I thought it best not to say things like, "I see an ax murderer chasing a kitten." Even if I did.

Image by image, I smiled, pretended to think for a moment, then answered: "I see heaven and tiny cherubim." "I see baby Jesus playing in a sandbox—with a puppy." "I see the Apostle Paul having lunch with Billy Graham." I'm not sure what the therapist scribbled down, but more than likely it was "this girl thinks she's a comedian."

My point is that there are many ways to see the world. More important, you can change how you see it.

Our human perspective tends to be at the microscopic level—so limited and narrow. Yet with a simple shift in perspective, we can get a completely different view. For example, as preachers we've been trained to come at Scripture and the craft of preaching with a somber lens. Professor Harvey Cox of Harvard Divinity School explained it like this: "The truth may very well be that we have inherited a recently perverted form of Christianity, that its terrible sobriety is a distortion of its real genius, and that a kind of playfulness lies much closer to its heart than solemnity does."[1]

This somber perspective on Scripture is a bit like the outside of my apartment windows in New York City. It is almost impossible

---

1. Harvey Cox, *The Feast of Fools* (Cambridge: Harvard University Press, 1969) 54.

to keep them clean, which means that I have to look at my Weather Channel app to see if it's cloudy or sunny.

So too, we as Christians have inherited a tradition where the dirty window of solemnity has become the reality. Humor has been excluded from our tradition for so long that we have simply come to believe the word is shrouded in a light brown haze of seriousness, that its seeming absence from Scripture is organic to our tradition.

Maybe we need to "do" some windows. One of the easiest ways to clean the window is to look beyond the surface of biblical words. The most disrespectful thing you could do as a preacher, an artist, and a human being is take a one-dimensional approach to the brilliantly creative, wonderfully rich book known as the Bible. If you stop on the surface, you've gutted the life out of it.

I grew up with literalists, so I know that some of you may be hyperventilating after reading the paragraph above. I'm not saying God wasn't involved in the creation of Scripture. I'm simply saying that God also gave us a brain. As one of my seminary professors once said, "To think is to worship God with one's mind." Sometimes, we need to change perspective to see the deeper meaning.

Move It!

Methinks that the moment my legs begin to move, my thoughts begin to flow.

—Henry David Thoreau

Another way to shake up our creative thinking is to literally shake it up by moving. Movement is directly linked to inspiration, and it must be part of our daily routine as creative thinkers. Walking is one of the easiest ways to achieve this. Studies have shown that walking brings clarity of thought, better memory, improved attention, and innovation. It also integrates the brain, synchronizing the left and right hemispheres responsible for logic and  creativity respectively. Holly Walsh, a BBC stand-up comedian/TV and radio writer, explained it this way: "Move around. You'd be surprised how many problems are solved walking to and from the loo. So drink plenty of tea."

You don't have to be Forrest Gump and walk or run for three years, two months, fourteen days, and sixteen hours. You could simply walk to the next room or around the block or into the shower, where some of life's greatest inspiration can emerge. If you are feeling lazy, then let something else move you. In fact, when I face writer's block, I sometimes jump on a subway or cross-town bus to jar my thinking. A change of scenery can change everything—especially our basis of inspiration.

I once read that you should live where you pray best. Amen. But I'll add something to it: "You should live where you pray and create best." Well, then, I'll take a ranch in Montana with a trout stream, thank you. The problem is that my beloved Madison Avenue Baptist Church ain't in Montana. It's in midtown Manhattan. So those of us who can't manage to live where we pray and create best have to find the next best thing.

For me, "Plan B" is to find trees, water, and sky. So I'll walk to the East River or stroll through Madison Square Park. Occasionally, when I have the time, I'll jump on my Harley and ride under a big open sky. Find where you are most inspired, and if at all possible, get there fast! Even if you can't get to your ideal place, shake up your setting a little and see what happens.

Go Ahead and Covet!

The human race has only one really effective weapon and that is laughter.

—Mark Twain

I know Moses carved a thing into a tablet about not coveting thy neighbor's stuff, but sometimes it's the best thing you can do. Cross-discipline study is one of the most productive ways to shake up your thinking. For example, Serena Williams once explained that she studied the footwork of heavy weight champion Muhammad Ali for her tennis game. Another example is the French painter Delacroix, who drew his inspiration from the literary world of Goethe and Shakespeare.

To shake it up as a preacher, I study all types of disciplines. For example, I study chefs. And why not? We preachers are in the food business. As Jesus said in John 6:35, "I am the bread of life. Whoever comes to me will never go hungry, and whoever believes in me will never be thirsty."

The chefs of the food world are some of our most cutting-edge artists. In watching a chef pair surprising new ingredients to highlight a familiar dish, I am inspired to pair  unexpected images to highlight a familiar Scripture. What could be more relevant for a preacher than lessons on new ways to prepare familiar food, creative ways to present the food, and, most important, how to encourage people to want to eat the food? Check out a new trend called "gastrodiplomacy" where food is used for fostering reconciliation and international peace building.

I also study storytellers. Listening to traditional storytellers like Fred Craddock, artists from the National Storytelling Festival, or spoken-word poets like IN-Q or one of the many talented rap preachers, offers a critical lesson in conveying images and ideas.

Storytellers follow the adage "show, not tell" by harnessing the power of detail. We should learn from that. Detail   is funny! For example, "a block of Velveeta" is funnier than simply saying "cheese." When telling a story or a joke, use specific names;

describe things using all five senses (colors/shapes, sounds, smells, taste, touch) so that the listeners can feel that they are there in the moment.

Storytellers are also expert tension builders, setting up their sagas by weaving in rising action until the climactic moment of success or failure. This not only teaches us the critical elements in telling a story but also shows us a powerful model for structuring a sermon (inductive or deductive). Perhaps the most important lesson from a storyteller is knowing how and when to end so that listeners will leave not only satisfied but also changed.

One of the best ways to connect with storytellers and other interesting new areas of study is to listen to podcasts. When I ask people over age forty what podcasts they listen to, I usually get a puzzled look. "Podcasts?" they wince. "Isn't that like listening to old-school radio?" Answer: no. Podcasts are to old-school radio as a Lamborghini is to a used Toyota Yaris.

Scroll through iTunes podcasts. Every imaginable topic is available in easily digestible segments. I listen to them in my car, on the train, at the gym. It doesn't matter. It's a quick way to learn and to see the world in a totally new way.

For example, I love one called *Everything Is Alive*. Written by producers from NPR, it is a series of interviews with inanimate objects. While the premise may sound ridiculous, the conversation gets into existential life questions in a hilarious and creative way. Like the interview with Louis, Can of Cola, who was wondering, "What's this all about?" thanks to his expiration date coming up.

It's a big world. Read about something new. Watch or observe someone or something unfamiliar. Listen to a podcast. By stepping out of our comfort zones, we clamp on our creative jumper cables and spark new thinking.

Exercises

1. Do you believe that you deserve joy?

2. What makes you laugh? Who makes you laugh?

3. How many times do you laugh during any given day? How much do you laugh at work versus home? Why? Is this something you want to change?

4. How do you shake things up? Where are you most inspired?

5. What artists do you enjoy watching or listening to? What can you learn from them as a preacher and a budding humorist?

Thou Shalt Learn to Write Like a Comedian

Humor can be dissected as a frog can, but the thing dies in the process and the innards are discouraging to any but the pure scientific mind.

—E. B. White

One of life's greatest miracles is the fact that small black letters carefully placed on a sheet of white paper can make people laugh. Examples of this miracle are everywhere. I remember when I was young, watching my mom reading Erma Bombeck, the nationally syndicated columnist, and laughing hysterically. (And my mother was a tough sell.) While their worlds couldn't have been more different— my mother was a Southerner from western North Carolina and Erma a Midwesterner from Dayton, Ohio—through the simple choice and placement of characters on the page, Erma's little 600-word columns made a total stranger laugh out loud.

That is where it all starts. Words on the page.

Some of you may be saying, "But I thought comedy was spontaneously made up." Sure, some of it is, like crowd work, improv, or riffing on a topic. But most professional comedians start with a tightly edited, carefully crafted set of words on paper. Of course, there are other things you add as a comedian to bring those words to life in a performance, like attitude, persona, movement, and facial expressions. The fundamental starting point, though, is words on the page. You have to learn to write like a comedian.

Punchline Goes at the End, Big Guy

A smile is a curve that sets everything straight.

—Phyllis Diller

One of my favorite movies is *Bull Durham*. Maybe it's because I attended college in Chapel Hill, North Carolina, and would frequent the Durham Bulls baseball games. And yes, I once saw someone hit the bull with a fly ball and win a steak. Living large.

Anyway, there is a great scene in the movie where the young macho pitcher "Nuke" Laloosh is hanging out with Annie Savoy, a metaphysical literary baseball groupie. Among the many pearls of wisdom Annie shares with Nuke is that the secret to great pitching is to wear a woman's garter belt under one's uniform. When he is later discovered wearing it in the locker room—backwards—Nuke is told by one of his teammates, "Rose goes in the front, big guy."

At this point, you are all thinking, "And this relates to comedy and preaching *how?*" Like great pitching, comedy also has a secret, and that is a punchline. And . . . wait for it . . . the punchline goes at the end, big guy. Maybe this sounds elementary, but you'd be surprised how many people screw up this most basic of lessons.

Let's back up a minute and start with the reasoning behind the lesson. While there are many theories on the cause and effect of humor, I'm sticking with the basics here: the incongruity theory. First articulated by Blaise Pascal, theologian, philosopher, and mathematician (a comedic combo if ever there was one), the theory holds that laughter is produced by a disproportion or disconnect between what one expects and what one actually sees or hears.

For example, we laugh at the proud person slipping on the ice based on the contrast of his or her dignity and the undignified plight. Or consider the contrasting images that produce surprise in a joke, like this one by comedian Emo Philips: "My grandfather died peacefully in his sleep, but the kids on his bus were screaming." For those of you wincing at the previous example (I winced and loved it at the same time), how about an example that is less risky to the kids—the familiar "peek-a-boo" game. We've all played it. The child sees you, you hide, and then you pop back out. It's the unexpected reappearance that creates the moment of surprise and consequently the laughter.

In comedy writing, the classic way to replicate that moment of surprise through words is with what's called a Rule of Threes or a Comic Triple. You set a pattern using two short, edited observations (the "setup"), then break the pattern with the punchline. Here's an example:

> I believe we are children of a God with a sense of humor. Consider the diversity of creation: heaven and earth [observation #1], platypus and blowfish [observation #2, and the pattern is set], Jerry Springer and Jerry Falwell [observation #3, which breaks the pattern and causes a surprise and—hopefully—a laugh].

Or consider my sermon opener from a Sunday after one of the presidential debates of 2016, where almost every candidate said God told them to run for office.

> This week I got to thinking about perspective [observation #1]. Or maybe God started me thinking about perspective [observation #2, pattern set]. Although after the presidential debate last week, I'm a little hesitant to say God spoke to me about anything [punchline].

It works because of the tension built with the first two items, which is then released with the third.

It's so simple, yet many people mess up this basic lesson. First, they give away the punchline. Newbie comedians love to preface their joke with, "Oh, this is so funny," or "Check out this joke," or "You're not going believe it, but this really happened." Now your audience is expecting a twist—something funny. And right there, the tension is destroyed. Wah. Wah.

They also tend to bury the punchline. This applies to comedy and non-comedy writing. When I say "punchline" here, I don't necessarily mean a funny punchline. It could also involve highlighting the point/ punch of your message.

On the micro level, consider basic sentence structure. Place your main point in a place that's not buried by extraneous material. Here's an example from the introduction in a recent sermon. I initially wrote it like this: "There was a forty-degree weather change in New York City yesterday. There was a guy wearing a wool turtleneck and cotton shorts walking down the street when I went out for lunch!"

But upon the rewrite, I shifted the punchlines (or main points) to the end of the sentences to ramp up their impact: "Yesterday, in NYC, there was a forty-degree weather swing. When I went out for lunch, there was a guy walking down the street wearing a wool turtleneck and cotton shorts!"

While this is a subtle difference, the slight shift focuses the "punch" on the important parts: the forty-degree weather swing and the wool turtleneck and cotton shorts.

It's also true on the macro level. In the story arc of the sermon, put the punchline at the end. This could mean at the end of the paragraph, the end of the story, or even the end of the sermon. And by this I'm not taking sides in the deductive (point up front) versus inductive (point arrived at the end) debate. In fact, you may well have multiple punchlines throughout your sermon. But wherever they fall, it's all about putting the most important material in a place that isn't obscured by extraneous words or ideas.

Jesus Was a Country Music Star

Humor must not professedly teach, and it must not profess- edly preach, but it must do both if it would live forever.

—Mark Twain

Back in the day, I wanted to be a country music star. I took the usual steps toward that goal: I bought a guitar, joined a songwriting group, and dyed my hair red. While I never made it to the Grand Ole Opry, the one thing I did learn was an invaluable formula for communicating an idea people would remember: a universal message hooked onto a memorable visual.

Here are a few of my favorite examples from country music titles:

"I'm the Only Hell Mama Ever Raised"
"Thank God and Greyhound You're Gone"
"I'd Rather Pass a Kidney Stone than Another Night with You"
"I've Been Roped and Thrown by Jesus in the Holy Ghost Corral"

If Jesus were around today (which he is—but you know what I mean), he would *definitely* be a country music star. He consistently hooked universal messages onto memorable visuals, like judging others linked to the image of someone who complains of a speck in their neighbor's eye when they have a log in their own (Matt 7:3). Or linking hypocrisy to a visual of someone giving to charity and then blasting a trumpet about his or her good deeds to generate honor in their favor (Matt 6:2).

The formula is easy to copy. Choose a story with a great visual that links directly to the universal message of your Scripture. Here's an example from a story I used in a sermon:

> Last November, my husband, Toby, and I decided to check off a bucket-list item and take Amtrak cross-country from Chicago to San Diego. As expected, it was a dream trip, complete with adventure, breathtaking views, and quiet time to read and relax.
>
> That said, by day three, our roomette began to feel cramped, and I started to feel (and look) a bit worn down. As Toby went to get coffee on that third day, I decided to surprise him by fixing up a little and adding a touch of makeup.
>
> When he returned, he stopped short in the doorway of the roomette, looked at me with alarm, and said, "What-is-wrong? You look so angry!"
>
> In that moment, I realized an important life lesson: Never attempt to draw your eyebrows on a moving train. Ever.

And presto, I launched from the story into a sermon about judging others from Matthew 7:1-5.

Here's another example from a parade I discovered in Whalen, Minnesota. It's called the "Standstill Parade" because the bands,

Shriners, firetrucks, and beauty queens are parked by the side of the road. It's the crowd that moves.

Seriously, if you can't preach that, then put this book down.

Now.

Perhaps even consider a change of career from preaching to filing documents for a large government bureaucracy.

I used this parade story for a fiery antiracism sermon that repeated the refrain, "It's our time to move" (see chapter 9). But the story would preach for almost anything. Why? Because it contains a universal message (taking action about something) hooked to a memorable visual (that goofy parade).

One important caveat here: Don't let the hook become your message! There has to be a tight link between the memorable visual and the message. Otherwise, the visual becomes a gimmick that overshadows the meaning.

In experimenting with this balance over the years, I have occasionally crossed the line. For example, there was a sermon I love to call "the chicken sermon." Fresh off Clown Camp (yes, that exists), I was dying to climb in the pulpit and try out my newly learned trick of folding a bath towel into a chicken. However, the link between the chicken trick and the message was weak.

To this day, people still say, "Wow, Susan, I still remember that chicken sermon. I just loved it."

I respond, "I'm so glad! What did you love about it?"

Long pause. "Ah, I dunno. The chicken, I guess? I loved watching you fold that towel into a chicken!"

In thinking back, I'm sure Jesus showed up a few times in that sermon, but that day he lost to the chicken. Had I framed it around a universal message like "don't judge because things aren't always what they seem," the chicken would have

taken its proper role and simply highlighted what Jesus originally taught.

This is equally true for sermon titles. They, too, need to offer a universal message hooked to a memorable visual. For example, here are some of my best efforts: on the power of patience: "Lord Give Me Patience and Make It Snappy"; on the need to pray daily: "Pray Like a Telemarketer"; on Earth Day: "If Mama Earth Ain't Happy, Ain't Nobody Happy." Ensure that your title not only is memorable but also reflects your underlying message.

Writing Like a Comedian and a Preacher

Life is serious all the time; but living cannot be . . . . [I]n your philosophy and your religion—you must have mirth. If you do not have mirth you will certainly have madness.

—G.K. Chesterton

There is a striking parallel between the formulas for writing stand-up and writing sermons. Let's start with stand-up. My comedy coach, Stephen Rosenfield, taught me four steps as the starting place for writing stand-up comedy:

1. Pick a topic you want to talk about (relationships, religion, etc.).
2. Put it through an emotional grid:
    • Things I hate about _____
    • Things I don't understand about _____
    • Things I love about _____
    • Things that blow me away about _____
    • Things I resent about _____
3. Create a short setup (with only one of these subjects), and try out different punchlines.
4. Collect and try out in safe places. See what people react to and edit down.

Let's try it. I want to talk about the church, and specifically the emotional grid of things that I don't understand about the church. Here are some thoughts:

- Why do some churches take the offering before the sermon?
- Why do we sit inside four walls to worship the creator of the earth and sky?
- Why are children excused during worship when Jesus said, "Let the little children come to me"?

Now we pick one and create a short setup. Let's take the second one and punch around a few ideas: "I don't get why we worship the creator of the earth and sky inside four concrete walls. Maybe it's because . . . the taller the building the closer to God? rain makes God's hair frizz? the cherubim are claustrophobic?"

Or you can try what I like to do, which is to "Mad Lib"[1] the setup. I take the premise and substitute different terms that are parallel in meaning: "I don't get why we worship [name a social gathering that honors someone] the creator of the earth and sky [name a great architect] inside four concrete walls [name a tacky structure]."

And *voilà*, you have, "I don't get why we worship the creator of the earth and sky inside four concrete walls. That's like giving a Nobel Peace Prize dinner for Frank Lloyd Wright inside Dollywood." (Sorry, Dolly.)

This formula is useful in sermon or speech writing because it teases out unexpected angles and unique perspectives. Let's pick the topic of loving your enemies, then put it through an emotional grid:

- Things I hate about trying to love my enemies
- Things I don't understand about loving my enemies
- Things I love about loving my enemies
- Things that blow me away when I have to love my enemies
- Things I resent about having to love my enemies

Pick one and play around with some punchlines or unexpected conclusions that will surprise your congregation or audience: "What blows me away about loving my enemies is that it's harder than I

---

1. "Mad Libs" is a popular game where you create a funny story by filling blanks with your own names and places in a preexisting story. I use a version of this game with Scripture. Try the "Mad Lib" with the Good Samaritan story in the appendix (p. 112).

thought, it can change perspective, it shows us how much we have in common, etc."

Eventually, you will arrive at a one-line summary of the message (which we will talk about in the next chapter): "Loving your enemies is difficult, but over time it changes your perspective by showing what you all have in common."

Exercises

1. Go back through your last sermon and see if there are any places where you buried the punchline. How would it improve the sentence, the sermon, or the overall message if you moved it to the end?

2. Think of some of your favorite personal stories. Can you link them to a universal message and make them preachable?

3. Spend ten minutes and work through the steps of brainstorming stand-up material. Then try a few of your ideas at the dinner table—or the pulpit. Afterward, return to the drawing board and polish up it. Repeat.

Chapter 3

Thou Shalt Get to the Point—Please!

Be bold. Be brief. Be gone.

—Callie Olson, 1st lieutenant and
chaplain candidate in the U.S. Army Reserves

Of all the pitfalls in being a minister and a comedian, the worst is being backed into the corner at coffee hour with no way out and hearing the words, "Oh, I have the best joke for you!" Instinctively, you know two things: the joke will not be that funny, *and* it will take way too long to tell.

Way.

"So, this zebra walks into a hardware store . . ."

Three minutes later as your feet begin to hurt: "And then he says . . ."

Five minutes later as you pray for mercy: "But none of them knew . . ."

Finally, at the seven-minute point, the punchline hits: "And the zebra said, 'Not weather stripes! Weather *stripping!*'"

A painful silence.

"Ya get it? Weather stripes—like a zebra?"

My Southern upbringing mandates that I muster some type of half-polite response. Crossing my fingers inside the pocket of my robe, I respond, "Yes, how clever. Thank you for sharing. I'm sure it will show up in a sermon someday," and I walk away in search of more coffee or something stronger.

We've all had this happen. Maybe it's the joke that takes too long to tell. Or worse, the email forward with the "re:" line that reads "This is SO funny!" Unfortunately, we all know those emails—the kind where you have to hold down the scroll button for ten minutes until you finally reach the punchline. Of course, at that point you don't know you are finished because you are lying on the floor sound asleep.

The adage is true: the longer the setup, the bigger the punchline needs to be. It's true in comedy and it's true in sermons. Yet we break that rule all the time. We have to—we have such important things to say. How can the world survive without our words?

Newsflash: It can. The world would be much better off if we cut what we say in half. At least.

Remember Jesus' words about prayer in Matthew 6:7: "Do not heap up empty phrases as the Gentiles do, for they think that they will be heard because of their many words." While the Scriptures don't specifically say it, I'm pretty sure Jesus then whirled on his heels, mumbled "snap," added a quick hand gesture for emphasis, and went on his way.

While we may think that we *have* to keep those extra pages because they are going to change the world, let me offer this comparison: the Gettysburg Address has 272 words; the Lord's Prayer has 66 words; and Moses saved an entire race of people with *4* words: "Let-my-people-go."

Just sayin'.

We ain't all that.

It's Judgment Day

First, you need a brilliant introduction. Second, you should have a dynamite conclusion. Third, be sure that your introduction and conclusion are not that far apart!

—George Burns on preaching

Part of the art form of editing is getting to the point—fast! If you think that proposition is intimidating in a pulpit, try it in a comedy club. In a club, there is only one point: laughter. You have to grab your audience in the first few seconds and make them laugh or at least want to hear more. Otherwise, you're done. Cricket sounds. And unlike most big, boxy pulpits, behind a comedy mic there is no place to hide.

While sermons and speeches *may* offer a bit more leeway, the same principle applies. You have to grab your listeners in the first few moments—clarify the relevance *to them* and make them want to hear more. Or you've lost them.

People make that judgment fast. Studies show that an audience will form a judgment of a speaker or performer in approximately ten seconds. Within that tiny time frame, they are asking, "Do I like this person? Do I trust this person? Do I want to hear more?" And sometimes the clock starts running not when you begin to speak but when your audience first sees you. Picture this: the Scripture has been read and all eyes turn to you—the preacher. You sit for a moment, gathering your thoughts, then stand and walk to the pulpit.

"Good morn—"

Boom. Time's up. You've been judged.

Let's be clear: these are not the congregations of our grandparents. I remember going to church in rural South Carolina with my dad's parents (Ganny and Grandad). Everyone would sit in the stifling heat, furiously waving their fans, and watching the preacher's every move.

At the end of the service, people would file out, and no matter how long (or bad) the sermon, they would shake the preacher's hand, saying things like, "Humdinger of a sermon, Reverend" (which I assumed was a compliment). But then again, that preacher wasn't competing with the global market.

These days, people have access to great sermons from all over the world, which means if this postmodern generation to whom we are preaching doesn't get what they need, they will simply change the channel, switch the video, or move to another church.[1]

Between social media, marketing sound bites, and thirty-minute sitcoms, we are trained to expect a tight, short, focused message. We are expected to communicate full thoughts, even inspirational messages, in 140 characters. And if that message goes off-roading to tangents unknown, then, as Tony Soprano would say, "Fuggetaboutit." You've lost your audience.

Here's a clue: if you find yourself conjugating more than seven Hebrew verbs in a sermon, you've lost your audience. Even if you are preaching at Oxford University, you've lost them. You have to ask yourself, "Is this necessary to convey my idea?" Please understand: I'm *not* saying you should dumb down the message. I'm saying you should be selective.

If you don't believe *me*, then believe the man who spoke the words we use to preach. Jesus spoke in recognizable language using familiar images in a short, concise manner. He targeted his message around the way people heard and understood information in his time. He focused on what they noticed, what they talked about, what they cared about, what they remembered. He didn't begin his messages with, "Hi, it's great to be back here in Galilee. Let me share a few things about myself, then walk you through the following ninety-seven PowerPoint slides on how to live right and make God happy." He jumped right in and hit people between the eyes: "The kingdom is like a mustard seed"; "For a rich man to get into heaven is like shoving a camel through the eye of a needle"; "What you did to the least of them, you did to me." Every single sentence a tweetable, 140-character message that has lasted over two millennia.

---

1. While young people are a focus of my discussion here, one thing that we don't talk enough about these days is bridging the generation gap and bringing all age demographics into the conversation. The older members can be invaluable in building a community of faith. For example, the most senior members usually feel the most ownership in a church, and while that can be perceived as a problem, try seeing it as a blessing. Transition their concept of "ownership" to "legacy," and help them realize their role—their critical role—in sharing the stories *behind* the mission with the next generation.

Jesus' words survived in an oral society for several centuries before they were written down. And isn't that our goal? To offer a message that people hear, remember, and ultimately *share?* Wasn't something said about that in the Gospels—go therefore and create disciples?

Some of you may be sighing at this point and mumbling to yourself, "We shouldn't cater to the demands and pressures of our postmodern world. I'm not changing my preaching to be popular or hip just to reach one demographic." Let me clarify something: this book is not about being hip or popular. If you want that, then move to Brooklyn. This is about harnessing one of the most powerful rhetorical tools available.

Extra! Extra!

Folks that think by the inch, and talk by the yard, should be shown the door by the foot.

—Anonymous

Here's a troubling statistic: audiences remember only ten percent of what you tell them.

Ten percent.

That's it. Even if you edit your content, your audience is still going to lose approximately ninety percent of what you say.

What do you want people to do or think or feel at the end of your sermon? What do you want them to remember? How do you make people remember? We need to get control of that ten percent because that is the whole ballgame.

The best way to do this is to focus your message, and you have to start from the beginning. When teaching this lesson, I usually ask people to write down the one-line synopsis of their last sermon or speech. Not surprisingly, many can't do it. The problem is that if you can't articulate the one-line summary, then trust me, your audience can't either.

Some of you may be saying, "That's not possible. My sermon message is much more complicated, more nuanced." Good for you. Enjoy your complicated, nuanced message because more than likely you are the only one who will, and you are definitely the only one who will remember it.

You start with a one-line summary. Write it at the top of your manuscript in **BOLD-FACED ALL CAPS**.[2] This is critical for several reasons. First, it sets you up for a title (or some form of your title). This is important because sermon titles can be posted on social media. They are what people see on the marquee when driving by your church. They are what some people use to decide if they are even coming in the door.

Second, the one-line summary underpins your entire sermon structure. For me, it is the hardest part. Once you get it, building the sermon is relatively easy. You identify two or three critical points you need to support that summary.[3] Then you link those two or three points with stories and details that have a memorable visual connecting to your one-line summary/universal message.

But there's one last piece: while being able to summarize your message in one line is important, it's equally powerful to infuse unexpected humor into that one-liner. Why? Because it helps people remember the message.

Medical studies prove the connection between humor and memory. According to Dr. Lee Berk, a medical researcher and professor at Loma Linda University, "The act of laughter—or simply enjoying some humor—increases endorphins, sending dopamine to the brain to provide a sense of pleasure and reward. These positive and beneficial neurochemical changes, in turn, make the immune

---

2. Here's another twist: Consider the Rev. Dr. Dominique A. Robinson, who has created what she calls "iHomiletic," a system that employs social media linguistics in preaching. Rev. Robinson suggests that we break down our sermon into a 140-character quote, complete with a hashtag (#) for the title and for the Scripture. That # or summary should drive the entire sermon or speech, especially in the writing process.

3. This is similar to mind mapping, which uses a diagram to visually organize information. It starts with a single concept in the center of the page. Then, associated ideas, images, or words are added, branching from the center. It is used by many in sermon preparation.

system function better. There are even changes in brain wave activity towards what's called the 'gamma wave band frequency,' which also amp up memory and recall."[4] Case in point: A Pew research poll showed that viewers of humorous news shows such as *The Daily Show* and *The Colbert Report* exhibited higher retention of news facts than those who got their news from newspapers, CNN, Fox News, or other sources.

We have to control that ten percent. And we can with a one-line summary, a bit of humor, and a creative yet structured message.

Welcome to Purgatory

Never miss a good chance to shut up.

—**Will Rogers**

In her book *Bird by Bird*, Anne Lamott declares that "we have to kill our darlings to make room for the truth." Yes, brothers and sisters, it's true: we are going to have to kill some of our beloved darlings—our life-changing paragraphs, our Pulitzer-worthy pages. We must cut them and put them in a place I like to call purgatory.

While I am not Catholic, I remember purgatory from reading Dante in junior high school. He described it (at least from what I remember at age twelve) as a place where souls go to work out their stuff on the way to heaven (like having a gym period before lunch).

Later in life when I started writing, I realized that I, too, needed a purgatory—a place to park the material that needed extra time to work its stuff out on the way to heaven (when it is hopefully shared or published). Now, in every writing project I type **"PURGATORY"** at the bottom of the piece in all caps, bold-faced, and underlined. When I find material that doesn't fit, I simply banish it to purgatory and wait for the right time to bring it back to life. I also (if I have time) do a document search for extraneous words like "really," "just," "good," "very," and "many." Especially if you are using that sermon for a blog

---

4. As quoted in Susan Onuma, "Loma Linda University researchers present four abstracts at San Diego conference," Loma Linda University Health, April 21, 2016, news.llu.edu/research/loma-linda-university-researchers-present-four-abstracts-san-diego-conference.

or written piece later, these words weigh down your message and need to go! (And by "go," I mean they skip the purgatory forgiveness category and are sent straight to the trash can to die a quick and humane death.)

Narrow your message to what is direct and necessary for your one-line summary, and park the rest in "purgatory." It's much easier to edit with that category because you don't worry about cutting material you like. You know it still lives. It's simply working its stuff out on the way to publishing heaven.

1. If you were giving your last sermon or speech on primetime, would people who were channel surfing stay with you after ten or fifteen seconds? Why? Why not?

2. Do a word search in your sermon manuscript and see where you use the words "really," "just," "good," "very," "actually," and "many." Delete them.

3. If you created a purgatory category for your sermon or speech, what material would come out?

4. Take your last sermon, presentation, or speech and write a one-line summary of the message. Can you do it? Once you've done it, compare it to the full text or message and see if that one line is reflected throughout the message.

Chapter 4

Thou Shalt Preach Like an EKG

Dear God, save us from the people who believe in you.
—Maureen Dowd, *New York Times*

I've always believed that a great sermon or speech, presentation, story, etc. should resemble an EKG. No, I don't mean your words should give someone heart palpitations. I mean that the flow of the message should resemble the pattern of an electrocardiogram.

We've all seen them:

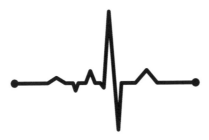

There's a spike, then a baseline, then another spike and another baseline, and so on. A healthy heart has a consistent mix of both. The opposite is a flat line. And we do *not* want that!

A power-balanced message must read the same way. Like a healthy heart, it must have a consistent mix of spikes and baseline, avoiding at all costs a flat line. Why? Because human beings have the attention span of a goldfish. According to an article in *Time*, Microsoft performed a study showing that, thanks to the impact of digital media on the human brain, adults tend to lose concentration after eight seconds.[1] The average attention span for a goldfish is nine seconds.

Bam.

You may be fortunate and find yourself in front of folks who can hang with your message a bit longer. But in general, our audience is goldfish.

So, short of fish food, how do we keep their attention?

Answer: constant change. That's where the EKG metaphor comes in. The spike in an actual EKG marks an electromagnetic change. The spike in a sermon or speech is similar in that it marks an experiential change. Change is what keeps people's attention.

Some have called it the "shiny object syndrome": anything new, fresh, shiny, or different draws human attention. We see it in infants who are attracted by bright light, primary colors, stripes, dots, and patterns. But once the child gets close and sees what the object is, they lose interest and start chasing the next thing. Adults are the same. Whether it's chasing the new gadget, new business idea, or new relationship, we're drawn to the next best, bigger, shinier thing. But when we get it, we tend to lose interest.

Comedians understand this as well. A veteran stand-up will deliver six to eight punchlines a minute to keep the audience's attention because in a comedy club the punchline is the "shiny" object. There is an expectation that you *will* be funny.

Not sort-of funny.

Not poignant, dramatic, well-researched, or interesting.

Funny.

It's an all-or-nothing game. The punchline is the only "spike" we have, and after the punchline, the audience loses interest and wants another punchline. And another. And another. It's like feeding a velociraptor.

That is the bad news for me and my fellow comics. But there is good news for everyone else: you have the sanity not to be a professional comedian. Congratulations! This means you have an arsenal of "spikes" at your disposal—not just a punchline.

---

1. McSpadden, "You Now Have a Shorter Attention Span than a Goldfish."

Three Spikes and . . . You're [a Knock] Out!

Preachers and public speakers have three categories of "spikes" they can draw on for their message: voice, content, and movement. Incorporate spikes in those three categories and you'll give a knockout performance.

Voice

The less people know, the more they yell.

—Seth Godin

There are multiple ways to create spikes with your voice. The most obvious is to change your volume. Mohammed Amer, my friend and Muslim comedy partner in the Laugh in Peace Tour, has a routine about being stopped by the police in his hometown of Houston, Texas. He explains that his uncle warned him that if he was ever stopped by a cop, he should speak Arabic. That way, the police would be confused and not give him a ticket. Sure enough, Mo was stopped. He began speaking Arabic, and the stunned officer responded to this foreign language by speaking slowly, yelling at the top of his lungs, "You-did-not-stop-at-the-stop-siiiiiign." After several more exchanges, the officer finally gave up and yelled, "No habla Español."

While volume does not necessarily help translation or clarity, it does get people's attention. Within any message, there are natural points where an adjustment in sound is appropriate—even required.

For example, when you lower the volume of your voice, you create an atmosphere of intimacy, a place where people want to lean in to hear. This can enhance certain material transitions, such as from fact statements to stories or emotional transitions, like from positive to pensive or even sad. If you choose to lower your voice, you have to stay close to the mic to ensure people hear you and get the full import of the effect.

Alternatively, when you raise your volume, you also signal a change—a spike. It may be that you want to emphasize a point, like our Houston highway patrolman, or that you simply want to wake up the crowd. And the mic exercise is the opposite. If you go louder, pull away from the mic so you don't get pops or harsh reverberations.

Speed is another way you can create a spike in your message. In some places it may work to speak quickly. Fast words charge the audience's environment, make them experience the tension of your story, and invite them into a feeling of pressure, rushing, even anxiety. That said, keep in mind that speed is fine, but your audience still has to be able to understand you.

Alternatively, when you slow down the delivery, the audience slows down with you. Their mental RPM revs slower. They relax. They *feel* the change.

You can also change voice. Rev. Dr. Fred Craddock suggested that we give voice to characters in our stories or in Scripture. To this day, it's one of my favorite spikes.

For example, I do a bit on how Southerners rarely have nicknames that match their given names. I start with the setup about the disconnect between given names and nicknames, then demonstrate by launching into a completely different voice. My favorite is one of an old line, old money, Junior League-loving, eastern North Carolina woman I once met who claimed she was related to members of the Lost Colony. In introducing herself, she said with a thick Southern accent, "My name is Sarah Louise Virginia Dare Dixon . . . but you can call me 'Fuzzy.'" I used that in a sermon about Jesus' crazy nicknames for many of the disciples.

Another example is a Christmas Eve sermon where I performed the noises of all the animals in the manger to demonstrate the title of my sermon, "It Wasn't Exactly a Silent Night." In addition to repeating a few of the noises throughout the sermon (see "callbacks" in chapter 7), I used the refrain "we are living in the chaos of a barnyard" to emphasize the anger, division, and disrespect within our world. The resolution was the universal silence that quieted the chaos when the babe was born.

No Voice

Sometimes you have to be silent to be heard.

—Stanislaw Jerzy Lec, poet

One of the most powerful ways to spike your sermon is no voice.

Silence.

Not what you expected, right? And perhaps even more surprising is that there are multiple types of silence.

For example, there is the silence in the pause before the punchline. Comedians use it to set off the point of their joke. Consider one of my favorite comedy routines on the Bible by comedian Dwayne Kennedy. He used silence to ramp up the impact of a double punchline in his Letterman debut: "I've been studying the Bible. And this what I have learned—two things that they talk about in the Bible *a lot*: wine . . . [long pause] and stuff that's hard to believe. [Long pause for laughter, then he adds,] I think the wine came first."

Any time you are about to hit an important point, pause and give a bit of air space for your message to hit. It breaks the pattern of your delivery and sets the core idea off like a punchline.

In addition to a pause, there's extended silence, which is a potent attention getter. Think back to when you were in junior high school. Perhaps there was a day you were bored, not paying attention, maybe doodling. (Not that I would know anything about that.) You continued to draw as the teacher's voice droned on and on. All of a sudden, you realized there was a silence. Slowly, you raised your eyes to the front to see that the teacher was staring right at you. The silence brought you back.

One of the most inspiring messages I've ever seen was offered through silence during the 2018 March for Our Lives rally in Washington, D.C. It was given by Emma Gonzales, a high school student who survived the shooting at Marjory Stoneman Douglas High School in Parkland, Florida, earlier that year.

Emma spoke only for a few minutes, then went silent. For minute after minute, she simply stood her ground, staring ahead, sometimes looking directly at the television cameras, and other times looking out at the thousands of marchers in the audience. After several minutes,

a timer went off, and she explained that six minutes and twenty seconds had passed, the exact length of the shooter's rampage. There was not a dry eye in the house. No one turned away. In fact, the crowd grew more and more engaged as the silence went on, shouting encouragement and chants. The media heralded it as one of the most powerful messages of its day. And Emma did it with silence.

The best way to bring a congregation, an audience, right back to rapt attention is to hit a big point and shut up. Say nothing. Or start your sermon with silence. Or put an unexpected silence in the middle.

Silence is one of the most powerful tools we can use, yet it's one we rarely employ. Why? Because it's scary. There's a reason we say, "Space, the final frontier." We are much happier hiding behind the wall of all of our important words. To stand still and quiet in front of people is threatening. There is nowhere to hide. Nothing to do.

And what about the sound-bite generation? Won't we lose them with silence? No—it's the opposite. They never hear silence. Ever. Taking five or ten seconds of quiet will be like introducing them to an exotic zoo animal. Bottom line: when you use volume, voice speed, or silence, you change the environment. You produce a spike.

Content

"People will forget what you said. People will forget what you did. But people will never forget how you made them feel."

—Maya Angelou

People hear and react to information in different ways. Aristotle explained that there are three modes of persuasion: logos (logic/information), ethos (character/credibility), and pathos (feelings/passion). Which one you emphasize should be driven by the composition of your audience. Unless you know your audience is 100 percent affected by one form (which is rare), then it's wise to mix in a little of all three. To present a sermon in only one form (logos, pathos, or ethos) is tantamount to a flat line.

Finding the balance is critical; you want feeling and passion, but your sermon needs to be more than an inspirational Pinterest meme. You also want scriptural references and appropriate exegesis and research. However, if logos and ethos were all that people needed, they'd simply stay home in their jammies and read the Anchor Bible Dictionary.

Congregations need more than they can Google. We have to give them what they *can't get* from the internet—we need to make them *feel* something in that sermon or talk. We need to tell them why it matters. In the end, the transition from logos or ethos to pathos, from facts to feelings, from pie charts to personal stories, is where a sermon starts to sing.

For example, you may start your sermon with a story (pathos), then move to exegesis of the text (logos), then quote a noted theologian (ethos), then perhaps add something funny to lighten it up and illustrate the point (pathos). Every time we change from one to the other, it's a spike.

We can also spike the content through how we *present* it. We can offer the information directly, or we can pose questions. Asking questions pulls people back in and engages them in the conversation. For example, if you are going to offer a surprising statistic (logos), say to the congregation, "I have a question. What do you suppose the percentage is of XYZ?" Maybe you solicit answers from them. That not only makes them think but also increases the engagement and the punchline—the impact of the information.

Movement

Speaking in front of a crowd is the number-one fear of the average person, even above death. So, if you have to be at a funeral, you would rather be in the casket than doing the eulogy.

—Jerry Seinfeld

OK, I'll admit it. I've always thought mimes were creepy. But then I watched a YouTube video about a group called Clowns without Borders and completely changed my mind.

Clowns without Borders brings performing artists to refugee camps, conflict zones, and communities who have experienced trauma or crisis. Due to language barriers, much of their work is done through clowning and mime. In watching them, I realized that the body provides all the language they need.

It could be a smile or a goofy dance. It might be a magic trick or telling a story through movement and symbols. Or maybe it's simply a change in facial expression. Whatever it is, the clowns cross multiple cultural, religious, and linguistic barriers to transform fears and sadness into joy—all through simple physical movements.

From vaudeville and Charlie Chaplin to the Marx Brothers to the British comedian Rowan Atkinson as Mr. Bean, movement and physical comedy have always been powerful tools of communication. But it doesn't have to be comedic. Any kind of physical movement informs our message. It can enhance (or undermine) our meaning. It also provides a powerful way to add a spike.

One way you can use movement as a spike is to simply move; move away from the pulpit, move from one point on the dais to another, or even move out into the congregation. (Be careful to use the latter only with congregations who are open to that level of intimacy and contact.)

You can also simply stand still and move your hands or your head. And no, I'm not talking about pre-set, artificial gestures. Do that and you look like a street performer doing the Robot Dance. Movement with your hands or head needs to be organic, emanating from the energy of the moment.

Growing up, I was a member of the Myers Park High School debate team. One Thanksgiving we had a tournament against the Bronx High School of Science in New York City. These students were the best in the country, and after watching the extemporaneous speaking competition, I knew why. The topic was global hunger, and the first speaker, a young woman, got up and stood in front of the audience in total silence. Not moving, she then began to snap her fingers every few seconds. After about ten snaps, she then stopped, stood rock-solid still, and simply said, "Every time I snapped my fingers, a child in our world had just died of malnutrition." Bam. She had 'em. And, most important, she kept them riveted for the rest of her ten minutes through a variety of spikes placed strategically throughout her speech.

You have an important message that can change people's lives. It deserves the best delivery method you can muster.

The EKG Test

Life is too important a thing to ever talk seriously about it.

—Oscar Wilde, playwright

Once you've constructed your message with the appropriate spikes, you need to give yourself a two-part EKG to test for flatlining. The first is for content and is done before the sermon is delivered.

In this initial test, I print my notes or manuscript and go through each page, placing a red check by the spikes in the text. Then I spread the papers across the floor in order and stand over them, looking at the manuscript as a whole. If you are more digital, then note the location of the content spikes on your screen. However you do it, it helps to see multiple pages at a time to determine if there are consistent content spikes throughout. Are they spaced? Are they too close together? Are they varied among logos, ethos, and pathos?

The second EKG test is given after the sermon or speech is delivered, and it is based on voice and movement spikes. For this you use a recording. Yes, I said recording. If you aren't recording your work, you aren't growing.[2]

---

2. You don't need expensive audio-visual equipment to record your sermon. A smartphone will work just fine. Buy a $25 tripod on Amazon, mount the phone in an inconspicuous spot, and hit record before the service. If you don't have a smartphone, then ask one of your younger members to use theirs. Otherwise, invest in a cheap video camera, which you can purchase for under $50. Bottom line: you have no excuse not to record your work.

First, watch the video without the volume. This allows you to focus on the physical delivery. How do you project on camera? Passionate? Energetic? Flat? Uninterested?

Second, listen to it with audio only. That helps you focus on sound. Are there vocal spikes throughout? Can you hear and understand what you are saying? Do you change up volume, speed, and inflection and use silence or pauses? Or is this sound best graphed as a flat line?

Strategically placing spikes throughout your sermon keeps your audience engaged and powers up your message and your delivery.

1. Do an EKG check of the text of your most recent sermon or speech. Is it an example of healthy communication or a flat line?

2. What spikes do you use, if any? How would your work change if you employed more?

3. Perform an EKG test with the text and video of Dr. Martin Luther King, Jr.'s speech, "I Have a Dream," and see what you can learn.

Chapter 5

Thou Shalt Find Material

I think I did pretty well, considering I started out with nothing but a bunch of blank paper.

—Steve Martin

As a stand-up comedian, I view the world as my playground. Everyday life is where I find the richest material. The comedian Steve Martin explained it like this: "Go to a busy public place and spend two or three hours sitting and watching people. Always listen and observe the world, as everything around you can be used in your comedy routine, skit, or screenplay."

The funniest things are in the simplest things. Comedian George Carlin, for example, crafted an entire routine around unusual words: "I insist that when you have only one M&M left, you have an M." "If you have twenty-five 'odds and ends' on a shelf and twenty-four fall off, what do you have left? An odd or an end?"

The comedian Jerry Seinfeld showed the world how hilarious mundane life could be  through things like detergent: "Now they show you how detergents take out bloodstains, a pretty violent image there. I think if you've got a T-shirt with a bloodstain all over it, maybe laundry isn't your biggest problem. Maybe you should get rid of the body before you do the wash."

Or birthday parties: "The first birthday party you have and the last birthday party you have are actually quite similar. You just kind of sit there. You're the least excited person at the party. You didn't even really realize that there is a party. Both birthday parties' people have to help you blow out the candles. It's also the only two birthday parties where other people have to gather your friends together for you."

As a preacher, our job is a bit narrower. While we have the world at our disposal, we must link humor in the world to lessons from the holy Scriptures. But then again, the Scriptures are funny themselves.

Humor in the Bible?

Is it possible, I wonder, to say that it is only when you hear the Gospel as a wild and marvelous joke that you really hear it at all? Heard as anything else, the Gospel is the church's thing, the preacher's thing, the lecturer's thing. Heard as a joke—high and unbidden and ringing with laughter—it can only be God's thing.

—Frederick Buechner

When I say that there is funny stuff in the Bible, many times people scrunch up their faces and say, "Really? Where?" I'd like to respond, "Can you read?" I don't, in reality, but I want to because so much of biblical humor is right in front of us.

The Bible spans the gamut of our human experience. It's a mix of everything from *The Real Housewives* to *Game of Thrones*. Frederick Buechner (one of the world's cleverest and most creative theologians) framed it this way: "Who could have predicted that God would choose not Esau, the honest and reliable, but Jacob, the trickster and heel, that he would put the finger on Noah, who hit the bottle . . . or on the prophets, who were a ragged lot, mad as hatters, most of them."[1]

I mean, who could forget Sarah and Abraham having a baby? Returning to our formula from chapter 2, here we have the universal theme of "hope" hooked onto the memorable visual of Sarah having a baby as a nonagenarian. Abraham falls on the ground, laughing at

---

1. Buechner, *Telling the Truth: The Gospel as Tragedy, Comedy & Fairy Tale*, 57.

God's statement that Sarah will be pregnant at ninety. But who has the last laugh? God. Because Sarah has the baby and Abraham names him "Isaac," the Hebrew word for laughter.[2]

Here's another example: in 1 Samuel 5:9, the universal theme of retribution is hooked onto the memorable visual of God striking people with hemorrhoids.[3] For this one, you'd better sit down (no pun). Yes, brothers and sisters, it's true. According to Scripture, the Philistines stole the ark of the covenant in a battle with the Israelites. In retribution, the Lord struck the Philistines with hemorrhoids: "The hand of the LORD came against the city, causing great panic. He struck the people of the city, young and old, so that hemorrhoids broke out among them" (1 Sam 5:9, The Jewish Bible, *Tanakh: The Holy Scriptures*).[4]

But wait—it gets better. The story goes on to explain that in order to rid themselves of the plague, the Philistines were forced to make golden images of their hemorrhoids, one for each of their idols. "Then said they, what shall be the trespass offering which we shall return to him? They answered, Five golden emerods . . . according to the number of the lords of the Philistines" (1 Sam 6:4). To see and understand this humor takes *zero* exegesis.

---

2. While many find this story uplifting, I find it harsh. I feel for Sarah. Whoever heard of obstetrics being covered by Medicare? No one talks about *that*.

3. This example is from my Old Testament professor, Dr. Alan Cooper of the Jewish Theological Seminary. In full disclosure (and continuing our theme of humor in religion), Dr. Cooper was also one of the original members of the band Sha Na Na.

4. This note is for you Bible nerds who want to wallow in the minutiae of the Hebrew translation of various body parts. In seminary, I did a paper on the translation of this passage, specifically the word "hemorrhoid." (As one does.) The original Hebrew is *ophalim*, which some Bible translations interpret as "sores," others "tumor," such as the International Standard Version, which translates it as "tumors of the groin." The King James Version translates it as "emerod," which is the Middle English term for "hemorrhoid." The *Tanakh* or Jewish Bible (Old Testament) defines it as "hemorrhoids."

Perhaps the greatest source of humor is from one of the best comedic voices of all time: Jesus.

Jesus? Jesus who?

Jesus Christ, people! (That would be an example of irony. You're welcome).

It's hard at first to think of Jesus as a comedian. He never laughs (at least in the text of the Gospels).[5] But you know he laughed. Seriously, how could he not?

We have information only on about thirty-five days of Jesus' thirty-three years. But in that short span, the Scriptures tell us that this is a man who shed tears, showed blazing anger, ate with sinners, was called a glutton, made up nicknames for his disciples like the "Sons of Thunder," and told pithy and clever parables about swallowing camels. And if that's not enough, his first miracle was transforming six jars of water (at 30 gallons each) into wine. Can we pause and do the math here? That's 180 gallons of wine! The gas tank of my Jeep wrangler only holds 19 gallons, and that'll get me from New York City to the state line of North Carolina.

While the traditional Gospels may not have Jesus laughing, the Gnostic Gospels do. In *The Sophia of Jesus Christ*, for example, Jesus laughs as he comforts and greets his disciples: "'My peace I give to you!' And they all marveled and were afraid. The Savior laughed and said to them, 'Why are you perplexed? What are you searching for?'"

Some of the best evidence that Jesus was a great comedian is the fact that he preached with the classic tools of comedy: exaggeration, irony, satire, twists, and reversals. For example, to describe the coming of the royal kingdom of God, does Jesus use the great cedars of Lebanon like many of the other Old Testament writers? Nope. He uses the absolute opposite image: a mustard seed.

The irony of this is hard to miss. First, it's a tiny, humble seed when compared to the omnipotent, majestic image of the great cedars. Second, as any farmer would know, a mustard plant is the *last* thing you would ever intentionally plant. It is invasive, hard to control, and takes over plants in other areas of the garden. As such, it

---

5. On the contrary, many artists believe that Jesus laughed. Google "Laughing Jesus" on Pinterest. Warning: Some of these images are sketchy.

arguably violates Jewish purity laws commanding that diverse things be separated.

If that's not enough to get Jesus' first-century audience buzzing, he then adds that it will become a tree "so that the birds come and perch in its branches" (Matt 13:32).

Birds? What farmer in his right mind would want birds? Yet Jesus is describing the kingdom here, not only as a lowly seed but as a seed of an invasive plant that invites birds into your garden and in the end might violate purity laws. It makes you wonder if Jesus had been sipping on those 180 gallons of wedding wine. But, in fact, he intentionally used the irony. One way his message could be interpreted is that the kingdom of God is not tidy. It starts small, spreads into unexpected places, and invites people others try to exclude.

Jesus also uses exaggeration, another comedic tool. For example, Jesus could have simply said, "It's tough for rich folks to get into heaven. Have a nice day." But instead, he chose an exaggerated image: a lumbering, smelly, surly camel being squeezed into the eye of a needle. Both images—camels and needles—would be familiar to his first-century audience. The exaggeration through the juxtaposition of the two images hammers home his message: "It is easier for a camel to pass through the eye of a needle than for one who is rich to enter the kingdom of God" (Mark 10:25).

Reversal is similarly common with Jesus in the Gospels. Indeed, the basic teachings of Jesus are fundamentally a reversal of established norms. Jesus tells us in Luke that the least among all of us is the greatest (Luke 9:48) and that the kingdom of God belongs to the little children (Luke 18:167-17). Similarly, Jesus sits at a banquet table with only tax collectors and sinners—those excluded by other religious leaders (Matt 9:10).

Another powerful tool Jesus consistently employed was satire. One of my favorite examples occurs in Matthew 5:40, where Jesus warns, "if anyone wants to sue you and take your coat, give your cloak as well." Theologian Walter Wink offers a fascinating exegesis of this passage, explaining that most of the poor in first-century Palestine wore only two

garments: an outer garment or coat and an inner garment or cloak. Playing on the image of debtor's court, a familiar and sore subject for much of his audience, Jesus says that if you are sued for your coat, you should give all your clothes to the creditor—in short, get naked in the courtroom. These words were particularly sarcastic given that nakedness was taboo in Judaism, with the shame falling on the person viewing or causing the nakedness, not the naked party.

There is great stuff in the Bible. You just have to mine it like a comedian mines the world for material.

Bringing It to Life

Sermons are found in stones.

—Rev. Dr. Frederick D. Haynes
(and Shakespeare's *As You Like It*, Act 2, sc. 1)

After my first year of seminary, I was fortunate to spend part of the summer studying under Dr. Doug Adams at the Pacific School of Religion in Berkeley, California. At the time, he was the one of the few (if not only) seminary professors in the country specializing in humor and the Bible. Professor Adams taught me that Scripture could be preached fresh every week if only we would do two things: (1) tap the creativity within its stories and (2) bring them to life.

He began our first class with the familiar Scripture, "Why do you see the speck in your neighbor's eye, but do not notice the log in your own eye?" But he didn't read the story; he told it from memory while holding in front of his face a large fake log that appeared to be coming out of his own eye. As he wandered through the class, bumping the log into people, he muttered things like, "Did you know you have something in your eye? It's very annoying! I wish you'd do something about it. I know that if I had something like that coming out of my eye I would certainly try to fix it!" In that moment, the story we'd all heard a trillion times came to life in a completely new way. And for a young preacher like myself, it was transformative.

Today, it's my modus operandi: finding the creative genius in the Scripture and bringing it to life. This is not everyone's way, nor should it be. But perhaps seeing a few of my choices will spark new ideas in your preaching.

To help with this, I've included excerpts of a few of my favorite examples in the appendix. Like the Pentecost sermon imagining that the tongues of fire experienced by the Apostles originated from them adding too much Tabasco to their dinner. Or a Bartimaeus sermon during the ongoing healthcare debate, which talked about how he would never have gotten healed today because he was uninsured.

I once preached an Easter sermon based on a spray-painted sign I saw in Memphis that said, "Trust Jesus and Elvis." I used the sign to link the resurrection story to Elvis fans because, unlike many so-called "Christians," Elvis fans truly believe the King lives!

Another Easter sermon was framed around parallels between the Easter story and major league baseball (Easter weekend coincided with opening day). The sermon title was based on a quote from Anne Lamott: "Grace Bats Last."

To deal with the struggle of describing or imaging God, I wrote "FaceTime with God," which imagines what we would see if we spoke with the Holy using the video chat app on our iPhones.

And after a particularly violent period in world politics, I delivered a sermon titled "In Re: God" (a legal term for "In the Matter of God") where I posed as the attorney representing the trademarked name "G-o-d." After one of our deacons posing as a bailiff yelled, "All rise!" and read the standard "Oyez oyez" to the congregation/jury, I used the sermon as a final argument against all who used God's name without permission to claim that "God was on their side." *That* was fun.

Still, none of these comes close to my motorcycle sermon about wisdom from the road framed around Elijah. And why would one *not* preach an Elijah biker sermon? After all, "[h]e was a hairy man and girt with a girdle of leather about his loins" (2 Kings 1:8).

You must see the creative gifts within Scripture and bring them to life.

Keeping a Humor Canon

The widespread failure to recognize and to appreciate the humor of Christ is one of the most amazing aspects of the era named for him.

—Elton Trueblood, theologian

When you work hard to identify the world's comic and creative gems, you have to find a way to preserve them. If you don't record things the minute they happen, you will forget. I don't care if you are seventeen years old or seventy years old. You'll forget. I promise.

To prevent hemorrhaging ideas, I carry a notebook with me at all times. If I see something that strikes me as funny or interesting or that will preach, I simply note the idea.[6] At the end of the day, I then comb through the notes (electronic or paper) and see if anything sticks. Sometimes, in the moment I'll jot something down and later think, "Nah, not worth it." But then there are things that I record thinking, "I'm not so sure about this," and later I realize it's gold. I keep these pieces of gold in what I call a humor canon. I organize it by topic (forgiveness, joy, fear, hope, second chances, etc.), and I go to it constantly for sermons, speeches, and comedy shows.

Comedians not only keep ideas but also keep their routines. I have a written version of every routine I've ever performed. While some of them are similar, there are always tweaks and changes that you may have forgotten. And those will be lost unless there is a record.

It's the same for sermons. Keep. Your. Sermons. And also keep a running record of the gems contained in each one. That may sound overwhelming, but trust me, it's worth it.

After preaching for eighteen years, I decided to do an inventory of every sermon I've ever written by topic, culling the one-line summary

---

6. Please understand that "notebook" can take many forms. Perhaps you like real paper. If so, buy a small Moleskine and carry it with you. If you are digitally savvy, use an app for note-taking and organizing. I use Evernote because it not only organizes things into files but also enables me to clip internet articles for later review. There are also OneNote and Google Keep. By the time this book goes to print, there will be 10,000 new ones. The best thing you can do as a communicator (preacher or otherwise) is to get digitally savvy. It is invaluable in the creation process, it will save you hours of organizing, and it will protect many a forest.

and pulling quotes, stories, or other gold that I might want to reuse. That involved more than 800 sermons. Yes, it took an inordinate amount of time, but now I have a store of my best material. That, in and of itself, was worth the effort.

It also increased my self-awareness in terms of preaching patterns. For example, it showed me that I tend to preach on topics like hope, possibility, self-care, and getting through the storms of life. In fact, after reviewing approximately 800 sermons, I realized that just about every sermon I've ever written reduces to four words: "God's got your back."[7]

Keep and analyze your material. It will exponentially improve your voice.

Thou Shalt Not Steal

The task of theologians is not to come to terms with existing patterns of perception but to explode them.

—**Professor Harvey Cox, Harvard Divinity School**

The phone rang one afternoon while I was sitting in my office busily trying to figure out a memorable visual for a Scripture out of Habakkuk. (Yes, I know.) Anyway, a voice said, "Susan Sparks?" which is usually not a good sign. The voice proceeded to tell me that they represented the ethics board of a major denomination and that one of their pastors had preached a sermon of mine word for word (including using my grandmother's name as their own grandmother).

Without my permission.

At Easter.

My first reaction was fury. Seriously? *Write your own material!* I thought. But my anger quickly melted to pity when I later talked to the

---

7. In *Craddock on the Craft of Preaching*, Dr. Fred Craddock suggests a more theological analysis by asking preachers to identify the central Scripture of their messages over the years: "There is a text of scripture that is so central to your theology and to your beliefs, so life-giving in its nature, so pregnant with meaning that all of your preaching flows out of that text and the implications of that text for your life and work. I propose that you identify that one distilled truth—just one brief text—one distilled truth out of which every one of your sermons come. And by which every sermon is informed and disciplined and inspired" (138).

minister in question. Finley (a suitably gender-neutral name to protect the innocent) was raw and honest, sharing that they were basically exhausted, stressed beyond measure, and facing a congregation that hated them and their preaching (or at least appeared to). "Just once," Finley said, "I wanted to see people smile back."

Ouch. What do you say? Does this make it right? No. But lord knows we've all been there.

My point in sharing this? Your sins will find you out. Whether in stand-up or preaching, no matter how tired or exhausted or stressed or judged you feel, *write your own material.* As Benjamin Errett, author of *Elements of Wit,* explained, "There are two types of people. Parrots and magpies. Some people just steal their lines and repeat them. Others hunt out gold."

There are certain times when using other people's material is OK. I quote comedians in the pulpit all the time. I even might perform a few of their routines. But I always give credit.

You too can quote people, share their thoughts and ideas. Had Finley asked me, I'd have gladly given permission for them to preach the entire sermon with appropriate credit to me. The world is big enough and diverse enough and crazy enough to provide us all with material until kingdom come. Use your God-given gift of creativity and craft your own message.

1. Where do you look for material?

2. Write down three to five funny things every day. Are there any observations you could use in your sermons?

3. Where do you find humor in the Bible?

4. Do you believe that Jesus laughed? Why or why not? How would it change your preaching if you believed that he did? If you could hear his laugh ringing throughout his parables?

5. Do you keep a record of your sermons? How? Do you review them? How often? How would it help you?

6. If you distilled one theme from all your sermons, what would it be? What is your central Scripture?

Chapter 6

Thou Shalt Not Be a Victim of Identity Theft

To refuse to use one's own language is to refuse to accept one's self, one's words . . . . It is a clear evidence of a lack of faith.

—**Rev. Dr. Fred Craddock**, from
As One without Authority

Identity theft is alive and well these days. Scary, faceless people lurk on the dark web, stealing our identity through our Facebook account, our credit card numbers, or our Social Security data. But there is another type of identity theft that is as prevalent: the world's theft of our unique identity as human beings. Those thieves come in many forms. As a comedian, the one nearest and dearest to my heart is the dreaded heckler.

The Dreaded Heckler

If you don't know who you are, you act like who you ain't.

—**Rev. Dr. Roy Medley**

Every comedian has experienced the dreaded heckler—the person who lives to tear down a performer. They wait in dark corners for the right moment to strike, yelling things that cut to the heart of your confidence: "You're not funny," "Keep your day job," or, my personal favorite that I heard from a patron at a comedy club in the Lower East Side, "Just let us drink in peace."

Hecklers are an odd breed. They are people who are either (a) insecure, (b) frustrated/jealous closeted comedians who don't have the guts to get onstage themselves, (c) generally angry, or (d) all of the above.

Tragically, the dreaded heckler is not limited to dark, smoky comedy clubs. We all have one in our lives. It could take the form of a congregation member who finds fault with everything you do.[1] It could be a business colleague whom you find intimidating. It could be a coworker or teacher who constantly focuses on the negative. Whatever form, it's the same formula—people who are (a) insecure, (b) frustrated/jealous because they don't have the guts/courage to do what we are doing, (c) generally angry, or (d) all of the above.

We are exposed to these negative voices from the day we are born. And sadly, over time, we tend to absorb their corrosive messages. It only takes one to sink in and the damage is done. The heckler then takes permanent residence in our head, waiting in the dark corners of our psyche for the right moment to strike with messages that cut to the heart of our confidence, saying things like, "You aren't good enough," "You're going to screw up," "You're aren't funny," "You aren't smart," "Who are you to say this?" or "People are going to hate this sermon." For a communicator, it can be the kiss of death.

Heckler in the House

Let the world know you as you are, not as you think you should be because sooner or later, if you are posing, you will forget the pose, and then where are you?

—Fanny Brice, comedian and actress

A colleague used to teach what he called the 3 B's: believe-behave-become. The voice we hear in our heads (what we *believe*) drives how

---

1. See Rediger's *Clergy Killers.*

we *behave*, and how we behave eventually drives who we *become*. When there's a heckler in the house, that trajectory can get ugly fast.

My preaching professor used to tell us not to mix metaphors. As much as I loved her, she's not present, so here's my mixed metaphor: a heckler in our head is like a bad virus. We catch it from others, and it infects us, takes hold of our system, and makes us ill. It poisons our confidence, making us doubt ourselves and question our ability.[2] In the end, we lose our voice, our personality, even our souls.

Voice Theft

The devil whispered in my ear, "You're not strong enough to withstand the storm." Today I whispered in the devil's ear, "I am the storm."

(Unknown)

As soon as we get up to speak, the internal heckler gets going, and once that negative monologue starts, everything reacts. The brain latches onto the negative message (believe), then transmits messages to the body to react (behave). We stop making direct eye contact because we're scared that people are judging us. Our shoulders slump as we try to subconsciously make ourselves smaller. With the slump, our diaphragm begins to collapse so our voice loses power. It also loses volume, as we are now speaking into the floor and not out to the audience. (Watch for these things in your EKG test!)

It's a vicious cycle. For example, in comedy if you start to shrink in any way, the audience will feel your hesitation. You have to commit to the joke or you won't get a laugh. It's the same with speaking or preaching. If you start to pull back in that pulpit, people will feel it and often start to pull back from you, in which case the heckler in your head gets louder and you shrink even more.

One of the worst internal heckler voice moments I had as a comedian was on set with *Naomi's New Morning*, a talk show on the Hallmark Channel hosted by country music superstar Naomi Judd.

---

2. One of my personal internal hecklers takes the form of a recurring nightmare: It's 10:58 a.m. on a Sunday (our service is at 11:00). My printer is broken, and I can't access my sermon. Or I've lost the sermon. Or my favorite—I forgot to write it.

I had been invited to help co-host with several other clergy. My role, as a comedian and minister, was to infuse humor.

It was the first day of filming. Having never been on a live television set before, I was petrified. We walked out of the dressing room and onto the set with its bright lights and live audience, then watched the cameraman point at the camera and count 5-4-3-2-1 with his fingers. Right before he hit 1, the producer of the show, who was standing beside the camera, pointed at me, then held up a handwritten sign that said, "BE FUNNY!" A second later, the red light went on and I froze.

All I could manage was a smile and a lot of nods as I listened to the other hosts join in the conversation. The voice in my head kept saying over and over, "You're not a *real* comedian," "You're not that funny," "No one will laugh," "Don't even try it."

The longer I went without speaking, the more locked down I became and the more frenetically the producer pointed at the sign. Finally, she began jumping up and down while holding it over her head. I stared straight ahead, silently begging God to open up my chair and let me drop through the floor.

We've all been there—that moment we get in front of a crowd and freeze. OK, maybe you've never technically frozen up before. But at some point in your life, you've heard the heckler, and you've watched your communication powers begin to sink like a balloon with three-day-old helium.

Personality Theft

When I stand before God at the end of my life, I would hope that I would not have a single bit of talent left, and could say, "I used everything you gave me."

—Erma Bombeck, nationally syndicated columnist

Back to our mixed metaphor. As the infection grows and the hecklers steal our voice, we start to hunker down and hide. We stop being vulnerable and authentic. We put on our masks, hiding everything but a sliver of our true selves out of fear of what the world would say or how it would judge us if it saw who we truly are.

One Halloween when I was six or seven, I dressed as what I thought was a scary character from *Scooby-Doo*. (I know, I get it. "Scooby-Doo" and "scary" are not terms that go together. But at the time, in my elementary school mind, they matched perfectly.) I proudly donned my "terrifying" outfit and marched next door to the house of my neighbor, who was nine and much older and wiser. After a few rings of the bell, he threw open the door, took one look at me, and said with great disappointment, "Oh . . . it's just you." My entire tiny body slumped over in shame.

It doesn't have to be a Halloween fiasco. We all wear our masks, our armor, things that make us feel safe, protected, accepted—even powerful. And we all share the same fear: the fear that one day we will be seen without those masks and deemed not enough. The fear that we will be found out.

It's a slippery slope. We worry about rejection, so we don our masks. But then, over time, we start to become like the masks. We want people to like us. We want to be accepted. We want our messages to be heard. So we subtly morph into things we are not. The tragedy is that in constantly shunning our gifts, we slowly shrivel and weaken from malnutrition of the spirit. Some call it the "imposter syndrome," the fear that we are not who the world thinks we are. Others call it shame.

Shame is corrosive; it eats away at us from the inside. It dictates our choices because we treat ourselves as we see ourselves. If we don't see ourselves as worthy, then we will drive ourselves into the ground in an attempt to become worthy. We will say yes to everything. We will fight to be the best at everything. We will destroy ourselves in order to be worthy.

Author and psychologist Brené Brown has written extensively on shame. In her TED Talk "The Power of Vulnerability," she defines shame as the fear of disconnection—the idea that there is something about us that, if other people know it or see it, makes us unworthy of connection. In short, if people knew who we were under the "scary" outfit, they would say, "Oh . . . it's just you." The

problem is that when we hide a significant part of ourselves, people stop recognizing us.

One Sunday morning on a cross-country drive before seminary, I stopped at a small-town church in Texas. Bubbling over with warmth and charm, the minister greeted me at the door with a lovely Texas accent. He made everyone who came in the door feel like they were the most beloved individuals on earth.

Then he got in the pulpit.

His entire demeanor changed. The man I met at the door was gone. In his place was a scary, soulless autocrat who stared down at the congregation with stoic eyes, shouting words of judgment and shame. He used words I'd never heard before, like "Jesus-ah," which I later realized was "Jesus" with an extra syllable for emphasis.

I was stunned. Had a UFO come down and beamed up the nice man I met earlier? Did we need a priest for an exorcism?

In my confusion (and my disdain for the Jonathan Edwards-esque sermon), I decided to sneak out the back door. Just as I was getting up, the sermon ended, and I could see his demeanor slowly shifting back to the friendly soul I met at the front door. When I walked out, he had returned to his old self, laughing and hugging people as they left.

We've all seen this happen at some level. You meet someone before an event and they're bright, funny, full of life and joy. But the second they get behind the podium or pulpit, the life—the authenticity—goes right out of them. They start speaking in a 1950s radio announcer voice. They use words, phrases, and cadences that you would never hear if you were at dinner with them. Their faces are flat and emotionless, unlike anything they would project to family and friends. Then the event is over, and they return to their normal, human selves.

It's a jarring thing for an audience to experience a person one way, then have a lifeless version of that person appear behind the podium or the pulpit. But sadly, that's the power of the heckler, and if that internal voice goes on too long, we eventually face total surrender.

Total Surrender

If you try and hammer a round peg into a square hole, you destroy the peg.

—Anonymous

The last stage of the virus—the long-term damage—is the worst. We believe the negative messages; therefore, we behave in a way that mirrors that judgment. And over time, our light starts to go out. Our beautiful uniqueness is worn down to a smooth, drab slab of homogeneity.

Once I was asked to preach at an Ivy League seminary. I chose a sermon that used storytelling and humor that played on my Southern accent. Afterwards, a young woman came up to me and asked in a neutral, flat accent how I had been able to advance as a preacher with my Southern drawl. Surprised (and a bit offended) at the question, I asked her why she thought it was an issue. I then discovered that she was originally from Tennessee, and within the first few months of seminary, one of the professors had warned her that to be taken seriously in the pulpit, she would need to lose her accent. *Her beautiful Tennessee accent.* Taking this authority as truth, she went to a speech therapist and filed down her ancestral, melodic notes to a foreign, flat, dead cadence.

This is how dreams get lost. This is the reason so many people fall short of who they hope and yearn to be. And the worst part? This is the reason that we then transform into the heckler of others. Because we are now (a) insecure, (b) frustrated/jealous because we don't have the guts/courage to do what we want or were born to do, (c) generally angry, or (d) all of the above.

How to Beat a Heckler

There is a vitality, a life force, an energy, a quickening that is translated through you into action, and because there is only one of you in all of time, this expression is unique. And if you block it, it will never exist through any other medium and it will be lost.

—Martha Graham, choreographer

My comedy coach, Steven Rosenfield, taught me that there are two ways to deal with hecklers: ignore them or annihilate them. Since this is a book targeted specifically for preachers, let's go with the first option.

For now.

Ignore

You're only given a little spark of madness. You mustn't lose it.
—Robin Williams

One of the best ways to deal with the negative tirade of hecklers in a club is to ignore them. They are looking for attention, for a shift of power from you to them. Silence is their kryptonite.

So, too, ignoring the heckler in your head guts its power. There is an ancient Native American story about a grandfather talking to his grandson. The grandfather explained that the grandson had two dogs barking at him at all times: a good dog and a bad dog—one on each shoulder. The grandson asked, "Which one wins?" The grandfather answered, "The one you feed."

As preachers, we need to realize that there is a quick and easy way to stop feeding the heckler and to be silent in the face of negative voices: practice what we preach. First, look at it as forgiveness. These naysayers are acting out of pain. Remember that those who discourage your dreams probably do so because they had their own dreams destroyed. As the old saying goes, "Mediocre attacks excellence."

You can also consider it an exercise in letting go. Lord have mercy, how long is the list of things we need to let go? How about worrying about making mistakes? There are three things that are sure in this life: death, taxes, and mistakes. They are going to happen. Rather than look at them as a negative thing, why not reframe them as a positive? A courageous act of risk-taking. A step in the direction of growth. As the jazz musician Miles Davis explained, "If you hit a bad note, it's the next one you play that makes it good or bad."

We should also let go of our fear of what others think. Our sermons, our messages, our communications to others are not a measure of our worth as human beings. There are seven hundred reasons why an audience doesn't laugh, react, or even emote during a message. Six hundred and ninety-nine of those reasons have nothing to do with you.

People might not laugh or react because they've had a bad day. Or maybe they are in pain, distracted, or exhausted. Other reasons may relate to you, not personally but as a speaker. For example, perhaps they missed your message or the punchline because you went too fast or didn't speak into the mic or slurred your words or framed the message in a way that was confusing. And let's not dismiss the possibility that your words hit them right in the solar plexus and they are simply trying to pick themselves up from the proverbial floor.

A few years back, I saw a young man in our congregation texting on his phone during my sermon. I approached him later and said, "Hey, you know I love you, but I was wondering if you might keep your phone off during the service?" He looked disappointed and said, "But Susan, I'm tweeting about your sermon." Ouch.

Their silence is not a statement of your worth. When we get up, our focus should not be on worrying about whether our audience likes us or our message. Our energies should not be spent projecting our insecurities. Our attention should be focused on how we can best deliver our gift of information, inspiration, and hope to these beloved people right in front of us.

Period.

The second we flip that switch, the hecklers in our head shut up because we've taken the focus off us and put it where it belongs: on our audience.

There is one thing, however, that I would not suggest letting go of—and that is nerves. Nerves are good. They bring focus and energy. And while you may think everyone in the audience knows you are nervous, unless you are balancing a tray of crystal goblets that reveals your shaky hand, they won't notice. If you want to let go of something, let go of your breath. No, I don't mean expire. I mean take a deep breath and exhale, intentionally imagining all the negative voices going out with your breath. That one simple act of letting go through breath lowers the blood pressure, focuses the mind, and puts a sock in the heckler's mouth.

Annihilate

Looking good is the best revenge.

—Tony Curtis

Even with the best tools of forgiveness and letting go, there is a point where ignoring the heckler doesn't work. That is the point you have to annihilate, which means two things. First, lower the cross hairs. In a comedy club, that means slinging some of your best "anti-heckler" lines right at 'em. Personally, I like "It's a two-drink minimum—not twenty." I also once heard a male comedian turn on a particularly loud angry, drunk woman and say, "Wow, you were nicer in the men's room!"

Whatever words you use, the purpose is to shame the heckler. It also harnesses the power of the audience. The crowd came to see you, to hear your material, not to listen to some drunken fool. Used in the right place at the right time, you can shut down the heckler and win the crowd all in one fell swoop.

After you lower the cross hairs, stand tall, hit them with your best material, and seal the deal. And I mean literally stand tall. Studies have shown that "power posing"—standing in a posture of confidence, even when we have self-doubts—can boost feelings of confidence and even affect our chances for success.

One thing I have learned as a comedian is that it doesn't matter if you bomb in the beginning of your set; it's how you leave them that counts. They'll forget the crickets if you leave them laughing.

The same is true with the hecklers in our heads. If ignoring the voice doesn't do the job, then you have to go for annihilation. I've found that cutting to the core of the internal voice is the quickest way to destroy it. For example, when the voice spews out some corrosive statement like "You aren't good enough," ask yourself, is it true? More than likely the answer is no. If it's no, then ask yourself, why do I continue to believe it? Why do I continue to carry this as part of my narrative? Who would I be if I let it go? By working through the questions, you gut the power of the heckler.

You can also harness the power of the crowd. You have people all around who hate the heckler voice trying to pull you down and who believe in you. They could be family, friends, other ministers, or colleagues. Whoever it is, plug in to their support, listen to them, feed off their enthusiasm, and leverage their power. Then stand tall and hit the heckler with your best material.

In the end, never let the heckler dictate your comedy set, your sermon, or your life. You have a powerful voice, a graceful heart, a warrior mind, and a joyous soul. These are God's gifts. Show up in all your fullness and raw authenticity, daring anyone to rein you in. And in the quiet realms of your heart where the heckler used to dwell, let this mantra ring:

I'm not going to tone it down.
I'm not going to blend in.
When I climb into a pulpit . . . you'll know it.

1. Who are your hecklers? Why do they haunt you?

2. What do they say? What, if any, nightmares do you have about preaching?

3. Who would you be if you ignored those voices, if you showed up in all your fullness and raw authenticity? Would you still be loved?

4. What would you be like as a preacher if you shut down the voices and hit them with your best material?

5. Please take a moment and enjoy a little inspiration from one of my favorite poems, "George Gray" by Edgar Lee Masters.

Thou Shalt Throw a Party

The Christian church has all the language of a party but hasn't been able to pull it off.

—Cal Samra

I've always thought that crafting a great comedy set or creating a successful church service is like throwing a cocktail party—which is ironic, given that I'm a Baptist. But hear me out.

When planning a party, you think about the guests: what they like, what they don't, what they might have in common. On the day of the party, you don't lock the front door. You stand there and greet the guests as they arrive. You welcome them with delicious food and engaging conversation. After the party, you follow up by sharing photographs, emails, or whatever will encourage your guests to remember their experience and return. Throughout the entire process, you add personal touches that make your guests feel special, like they matter more than anything else. Why? Because *you* invited them.

Those are the same goals we should have for our congregations or any audience. Whether it's a religious service, a comedy club, a board meeting, a keynote speech, or a jury argument, you are the host. You issued the invitation. And for the "party" to work, it has to be all about your guests.

Pre-Party Planning

Question: How does NASA organize a party?
Answer: They planet.

Any seasoned host or hostess will spend a significant amount of time thinking about the guest list. Who is coming? What are their names? What do they enjoy? What are their interests? What makes them tick? Who would enjoy meeting whom? You have to know who is coming in order to know how to engage and serve them.

A congregation or audience is the same way. One of my business partners, Steven Mann, used to say, "Put yourself behind the eyes of the audience before you put yourself in front of them." This is great advice. Know your audience—know what they need, what they want, what they worry about, what wakes them up in the middle of the night, what they dream about—before you step in front of them.

Without adequate research about your audience, you may well offer material that they don't understand or care about. Many years ago, I was the speaker for a high school church retreat in western New York State. One of the sessions was dedicated to funny things in the Bible. At the end, I marched out my all-time favorite Scripture, discussed in chapter 5, where God struck the Philistines with hemorrhoids. While the adult audience members laughed hysterically, the students were deadly silent. Finally, a young man raised his hand and said, "What's a hemorrhoid?"

Duh. Like a high school student would know.

Even with carefully targeted material, you also need to know how to pitch it. For example, a late-night audience in a comedy club in the Lower East Side of Manhattan will not necessarily appreciate the same pitch as one at the Elks Club in Devils Lake, North Dakota. (Personally, I would prefer to perform in Devils Lake.)

Case in point: Part of my comedy routine is a description of a Southern greeting. While funny, it needs to be pitched differently to Southern audiences than to everyone else. For example, if I am in front of a Southern audience, I introduce it by saying something like this: "I so

miss the South. Especially how polite everyone is—even to the point of how we greet each other. Y'all know what I'm talking about . . . ." And with that, I'm in. That introduction bonds us as Southerners, with our mutual love of our colorful culture.

Alternatively, when I am outside the South, I take the opposite approach and highlight the wacky nature of the greeting by saying something like, "The transition from the South up North has been so hard! I didn't realize how crazy we Southerners talked. Like how we greet each other . . . ." Again, I've bonding with the audience, but this time by laughing *with* them *at* me.

Understanding your audience also protects you from unreasonable expectations. One time, I did a comedy show for a large Lutheran audience in the Midwest. For more than thirty minutes, I offered tried and true material that always got a laugh. Nothing. Nada. Crickets. Finally, I hit them with my best line at the end, and there were a few head nods and one muffled giggle from the back. I left the stage utterly dejected.

A few minutes later, one of the organizers came to me and said, "Susan, that was amazing! The best we've ever had."

I looked at him in confusion. "But they were so quiet!"

He laughed and said, "A smile and a head nod are the Lutheran version of a standing ovation."

The irony is that I later married a Lutheran. Go figure.

There are those who may read this and say, "I refuse to target my message to what people *want* to hear." I am charged with speaking truth to power, changing people, shaking people from their stagnation.

I have two responses. First, have you read the parables of Jesus? I'm curious, since they are all brilliantly tailored to their first-century audience.

Second, have fun on your self-righteous journey. If you refuse to know and speak to your audience, then either you are preaching to a congregation with a worldview as narrow as a slot canyon, or you are preaching to no one. Either way, it's utterly ineffective.

I believe my job as a pastor is to encourage people to think, to argue, to read, and to learn. I, too, want to inspire people toward change, but in order to do that, I have to first secure their trust and speak their language. And the way to do that is to know your audience.

One way I try to do this is to imagine my congregation as I am crafting a sermon. As I write, I see in my mind's eye the person who sits in the back and is fighting stage 3 cancer, the Baby Boomer who has recently lost a job, the mom whose teenager is acting out, the teenager who is fighting depression and anxiety, the elderly woman who is alone, the recent immigrant who knows no one in this country. I see them, and I think about what keeps them up at night. Then I return to the Scripture I'm working with to see it through their lens.

The best pre-party planning: Know. Your. Audience.

Day-of-the-Party Planning

From sour-faced saints, good Lord, deliver us!

—St. Teresa of Avila

A. Greet them at the door.

Be so good they can't ignore you.

—Steve Martin

When you throw a party at your house, you don't simply leave the front door unlocked with a handwritten sign that says, "Come in." You welcome people *at the door.*

In other words, you set the tone.

It's the same if I'm giving a keynote or doing a comedy show. I don't wait for the audience to set the tone. *I* set it. I'm greeting people as they come in the door. I'm chatting with people at their tables. By doing so, I'm putting good will in the bank. I'm branding an invaluable imprint with them before I even start. Remember in chapter 1 where we talked about people judging us in the first ten seconds? This is the way to preempt that judgment.

It's the same (or should be) at church. Standing at the front door and welcoming your guests is not only the right and polite thing to do; it's the savvy thing to do. It creates an atmosphere of welcome and intimacy. And with the postmodern millennial crowd, authenticity and hospitality are the entire ballgame.

It's also what many of them need. In my church, many of the younger visitors who walk in our doors for the first time have been wounded through ecclesiastical judgment and shame. You name it, they've been through it. Yet, miraculously, these injured folks are somehow drawn back. It's an extraordinary act of courage, and one that demands an immediate prodigal-son welcome from a representative of the institution that inflicted the harm.

That's why the first things they receive from our ushers, our members, and me are a smile and a word of greeting. Upon receiving those signs of welcome, their shoulders drop, they return the smile, and they enter our doors willingly, which means they enter with open hearts ready to hear the message. A representative of the church, standing outside the door, plows the ground. And with a little rain, you never know what can grow.

It's astonishing to me that many pastors don't take advantage of this critical opportunity. Some say they can't because they need the preparation time. Newsflash: If your thoughts aren't collected within thirty minutes of the time when you'll go onstage or start preaching, then you will never be "collected." Please understand that I say this as the world's premier procrastinator, but our potential unpreparedness has to be balanced against the rocket-fuel type of power of being present at the door.

Other folks might say, "Well, I'm an introvert, and standing out front is not my thing." Or "I'm tired and don't have the energy to do any more face to face than is absolutely necessary." I get it. Jesus didn't always feel like putting on his game face. We know that because he was constantly pulling away from the crowds to rest. But in the end, he showed up—big time. And so should we.

Here's a twist: It doesn't have to be a literal door. There are many "doorways" at which we might greet people, and most of them are available way before Sunday morning. For example, we post messages on our church marquee that grab people's attention, make them think—and perhaps, even laugh. Favorites include "What happens in Vegas is forgiven here," "The reason so many people get lost in thought is because it's unfamiliar territory," and "Honk if you love Jesus, text while driving if you want to meet him." Those signs invite people to engage with us. They cause people to pause for a moment and smile (even laugh). Passersby take photos, then share on social media. Some even come in out of curiosity to see what we're about.

Speaking of social media, Facebook, Instagram, Twitter, and YouTube are powerful front doors. Rev. Ned Lenhart, a dear friend and a Lutheran pastor in Wisconsin, has a great pre-service invitation that he posts on his church's Facebook page early each Sunday morning: "Coffee's brewing, band is tuning up, and this pastor is praying. We are Living Water, and you are welcome here." If I was looking for a church and found that on Facebook, I would pack up my entire family and head to Wisconsin.

Perhaps the most important front door is your website. It's the gateway to your community, so it should offer the closest thing you can manage to a personal handshake and a word of welcome.

It's about welcoming people at the proverbial and literal front door, but it doesn't stop at the door. It continues once the service starts, projecting positive welcoming energy from the call to worship through the benediction. God forbid you make eye contact with the congregation during the hymns and smile! If that feels awkward, too bad. You chose to be up front. Own it. You set the tone by welcoming people at the door.

B. Be a great conversationalist.

Sometimes the road less traveled is less traveled for a reason.
—Jerry Seinfeld

There are several core elements to being a great conversationalist:

1. Look them in the eye. We've all been in a meeting or at a cocktail party where the person talking to us is looking over our shoulder the entire time. Are they scanning the crowd for someone more interesting to talk to? Are they bored? Do they find us dull or dreary?

Whatever the reason, the experience can make us feel excluded, unimportant, and irrelevant.

There is no difference in that scenario and delivering a sermon or a message. Does our audience feel like we are looking right past them, scanning the horizon for better options? When we armor up with scripted words, keep our eyes glued to the manuscript, hide our true selves behind masks of formality, ignore the obvious things going on around us, and enter "robo-pastor" mode, our audience, too, will feel excluded, unimportant, and irrelevant.

Guaranteed.

One of the most important things as a comedian and a preacher is maintaining eye contact. First, let me define "eye contact." This does not mean looking at the floor in front of the pulpit or at the corners of the room above the heads of the people in the back row (which seems to be a favorite of many speakers). "Eye contact" means your eyes meet your audience's eyes.

I know, I know. Looking someone in the eye can be scary. But so is serving Communion for the first time and dropping the body of Christ on the floor. Hey, it's all part of the job.

For comedians and professional speakers, the power is in the eye contact. It's about trust and believability. For a comedian, especially, the kiss of death is to take a 5-x-7 index card on stage and read your set. Only rank amateurs do that. After that, you lose immediate credibility. The power comes from appearing to be in the moment— in a free-flowing, intimate, honest conversation with your audience. If you're reading, you lose that.

It's the same with a congregation. When you drop eye contact, it's like unplugging a power cord: the meter drops to zero. You lose intimacy and honesty. You also lose the ability to engage in real time with the audience. When you make eye contact, you see people's reactions and can react or comment if appropriate.

There are several ways to do this. Comedians usually deliver their punchlines to one person. I use a modified version of that in preaching with what I call quadrant eye contact. Throughout the sermon, I pick one person per quadrant of the congregation and lock eyes. Even though it's only one person, the congregation is far enough away that the quadrant around them feels that they are part of your gaze.[1] This is especially critical at the beginning and end of your sermon because (as you now know) the beginning drives whether they'll listen and the end drives what they take away.

Where the rubber hits the road for a preacher is the age-old question: manuscript or no manuscript? To me, there's no right or wrong answer. Preaching from a manuscript is as much an art form as going without. It's all in how you do it.

If you're going to preach without notes, you have to put in the work. In fact, the best non-manuscript preaching is ironically done after writing a manuscript. That way you ensure a tight, edited message with a clear structure.

I grew up with rural Southern preachers sporting giant, blow-dried, white-coiffed 'dos who would get up and rely solely, as they would say, on the Spirit. Let's just say they gave the Spirit a bad rap. I've heard Spirit-filled sermons. They can take a congregation and lift it through the roof. But the Spirit will only land when the work's been done. The sermons of my early days came across more like someone *drinking* spirits, given how they wandered, stumbled, and headed off into unknown directions.

If you are interested in manuscript-free preaching, consider the formula Joseph M. Webb offers in his book *Preaching without Notes*.[2] He suggests a specific week-long schedule to prepare. Monday and Tuesday are spent identifying your topic, preparing your one-line summary, finding the metaphor (universal theme with a memorable visual), and gathering your material. Wednesday is the day to frame your information into clear, distinct sequences or blocks that you shift around according to summary titles to find the final organizational structure. Finally, you spend Thursday and Friday setting the sequence to memory through repetition and rehearsal.

It's a fantastic system. The trick is to be disciplined enough in your week to follow the steps. Unfortunately, for many of us parish

---

1. Word of caution: Do not hit a point that involves sin or evil and lock eyes with, say, the chair of your Trustees Board.

2. I also highly recommend Professor Webb's book *Comedy and Preaching*.

ministers, our week spins off into unexpected emergencies and crises we can't predict. That's why, over the years, I've figured out ways to fake it—to use a manuscript but look like I am preaching without one.

First, I print the sermon in inordinately large print. For me, that means a particular font size. Whatever works for you. The point is that large words allow you to quickly glance down to catch the idea and immediately look back out to the audience.

I also make a little book. This may sound trite, but when you tape your pages together like a book, you don't worry about flipping pages or, God forbid, dropping pages from the pulpit. You don't look down as much. You can also use an iPad and scroll through your sermon. The problem for me with an electronic manuscript is that I can't do my second step: notating the text.

I do at least two read-throughs of my sermon, circling key words. This way I can glance down to catch the word or phrase and then look up without breaking much eye contact. I also add delivery notes, such as two slashes for a pause, or for a story I bracket the topic or keyword so I can share it without reading. By the way, never read a story. It guts all the intimacy and authenticity. Come up off your notes, and share the story in your own words. It's all about looking them in the eye.

2. *Be present.* One of the worst things you can do as the host of a party is to nod your head aimlessly in a conversation while your focus is somewhere else completely. We've all been on the receiving end of this. It makes you want to snap your fingers in front of someone's eyes and say, "Is anyone in there?"

That's why improvisation training is so important in stand-up. You have to be utterly present at all times in a show to observe and work with the world around you. And it's no different for a worship service. If something obvious or disruptive happens and we don't call it out, the congregation is going to feel like snapping their fingers in our face, saying, "Is anyone in there?"

Early in my ministry, there was an elderly gentleman in my congregation named Charlie McCarthy. Hilarious, I know. (For those younger readers, Charlie McCarthy was a famous ventriloquist puppet from the 1920s.) Anyway, Charlie always sat on the front row, partly because he was hard of hearing and partly because it was CbC (Charlie being Charlie). One Sunday morning, in the middle of a quiet, somber prayer, Charlie (97 years old at the time) yelled out, "Lord! Please help the Mets. They stink this year!" Several heads raised, and a few eyes opened and looked at the pulpit with questioning expressions. What choice did I have but to respond, "Yes, Lord, this year's team is awful. Do what you can." Then I continued on with the prayer about global starvation.

Another favorite example comes from a three-year-old sitting in the back of our sanctuary. While she held it in pretty well through the beginning of the service, right as I stood up to begin my sermon, she yelled out her new favorite word, "Uh-oh!" There was a momentary silence as everyone tried not to laugh. I could have continued without noting it, but why do that? We all heard it. It needed to be acknowledged. In fact, it was an unbelievable gift. So I said, "It's a bad start when you get up to preach and the congregation says, 'Uh-oh.'" The entire church burst into laughter because it bonded us over an awkward moment we had all shared.

Noting things from the service also can make great transitions. Once, as I started our Sunday prayer, an ambulance with the sirens wailing stopped at the light right outside the front doors of the church. I waited until it passed, then said, "Let us begin our prayers this morning with raising thanks that none of us are in that ambulance." The congregation laughed, but it brought home the point of blessings and helped bridge us from the noise into the silence. It's simply about experiencing the world in real time with the congregation and reacting *with* them.

3. Share the conversation. One thing every great host does is ensure good communication. That includes speaking clearly, slowly, and in a way that everyone can understand. But this should be a given. I want to talk about *truly* sharing the conversation.

One of the most annoying things a host can do is interrupt. A guest expects to get your focus, to be heard, and not to be disrupted in the middle of the story.

So, too, as a comedian, the kiss of death is to interrupt. In the business, they call it "stepping on your hold." A "hold" is the time immediately after you hit a punchline where you stay silent as the audience absorbs the joke and reacts. To "step on your hold" means to start talking too soon before the peak of the laughter. If you do that, the audience will stop laughing to hear you. It's like throwing water on a fire. It robs the energy of the moment. It steals their joy. In the comedy world, it is the ultimate sign of a rookie. It's easy to do, but it takes the air right out of a punchline.

Experienced comedians will hold until they get the reaction, then start their next line only after the laughter has died down significantly, but not fully. That is called "riding the wave." If the peak of the laugh is the highest part of wave, the hold should last until about the three-quarters point, midway down the backside. Some comedians even milk the hold by staying silent until the laugh totally dies, then using a facial expression or physical gesture that emphasizes the punchline, causing the audience to erupt in laughter again.

This is a critical tool for preaching and speaking as well. When you hit a punchline or a major point (either applies), you have to hold in silence as the audience absorbs the joke or point and reacts. Remember, while you may be doing all the talking, the message is still a conversation—one where you offer an idea and then wait to make sure the audience understands the point. Unlike reading a book, they can't reread what you just said or highlight it for later reference. You have to give them time to absorb it. That's the sign of a great conversationalist and a confident communicator.

Comedians also use a tool known as a "callback," where a comic will "plant" a joke early in the set, then call it back later. In my set, I plant a joke early using a popular Southern phrase: "Southerners have a little trick where you can say anything you want, about anybody you want, as long as you end the phrase with, 'Bless their hearts.'"

There will be a laugh, and then I go on to other material. Later in the set, I'll come back to it by saying something like, "Seminary was hard for me. Those professors weren't ready to teach theology to a comedian. [beat] Bless their hearts." The phrase gets an even bigger laugh at that point. Recalling a punchline bonds the audience, making them feel like they are part of an inside joke. Once again, it all circles back to creating intimacy and trust.

Callbacks can also be used for repetition of our one-line summaries to ensure the point sinks in. Consider Dr. King's "I Have a Dream Speech." The phrase "I have a dream" was used as a callback throughout. It is what his audience remembered. And it is what we remember even to this day.

C. Feed Them Yummy Food They Wouldn't Otherwise Get

Laughter is carbonated holiness.

—Anne Lamott, author

When I was little, we'd spend summers at my grandparents' farm in the North Carolina mountains near Brevard. It was located at the end of a long dirt road where you could see people coming for over a mile. Many a summer night, we'd be sitting at the table, eating our classic rural Southern meal of cornbread and buttermilk, when my grandmother would spy a dust cloud coming down the road.

"Som'uns comin'!" she chirped, then jumped up and headed for the kitchen. Next thing you know, she has our modest dinner cleared off the table, and smells of her famous biscuits, fried chicken, and creamed corn were wafting from the wood stove. Visitors were always welcomed at that home with great food.

Years later, I can't help wondering if Grandmother Whitmire was a secret Bedouin living in Western North Carolina. The parallels between her practice and the ancient Middle East practice of hospitality are striking. Exhibit A: Leviticus. "But the stranger that dwelleth with you shall be unto you as one born among you, and thou shalt love him as thyself; for ye were strangers in the land of Egypt: I am the LORD your God" (Lev 19:34). Or consider Exhibit B (and my personal favorite): "Be not forgetful to entertain strangers:

for thereby some have entertained angels unawares" (Heb 13:2). You see this ethic throughout the Bible.

Jesus knew the power of food. Think about the afternoon when he stopped along a hillside overlooking the Galilee. A 5,000-plus crowd that had been following him and the disciples gathered around him. The first thing Jesus did was not to grab the mic and solicit an offering or plug his book. No, he healed their sick, then fed them from only fives loaves of bread and two fish with food to spare. Jesus fed the crowd with food they would not otherwise get, literal food for their journey and figurative food for their souls.

So too we must offer food that our congregations or audiences would not otherwise get.[3] This means carefully prepared food, special food with meaning and heart that was specifically meant for them. They can find YouTube videos about everything from changing the oil in their cars to baking a soufflé. They can get TED Talks, Udemy lectures, and podcasts. What they can't find via media or online is a live person who has walked with them through good times and bad, who has baptized their children and buried their loved ones, who loves them into living God's gift of life and makes them feel like they matter, they're special, and they're not alone. That is not on the internet—and never will be. That is the food for which people are hungry. And that is the food we need to be serving.

Post-Event Planning

If you don't have anything nice to say, come sit next to me!

—Alice Roosevelt Longworth

After you give a party, one of the things people love to receive is photos, notes, or other reminders of the evening—something to let them know how much you appreciated having them in your home and how much they mean to you. It's like the ultimate deal closer. It

---

3. This brings up the issue of recycling sermons. Don't do it if you can avoid it. If you need to (and we all have), then make sure to update the examples, the voice, and the details. I once heard about a pastor who was asked to guest preach at a famous resort. He read an old sermon word for word, including the introductory words thanking the organizers . . . of a previous event in a different state.

cements friendships and relationships and leaves a warm feeling with everyone who came.

I do the same thing after every comedy show or keynote. I send a thank-you note to the organizers. I also follow up with any individuals from the audience with whom I've connected. There are several reasons I do it. First, it's the polite thing to do (says the Southerner). It's also a kind thing to do. Event organizers are usually overworked, underpaid, and underappreciated. A "thank you and job well done" note goes a long way. Finally, it's a smart business move. A follow-up can cement more jobs, emails for contact lists, social media connections, and recommendations.

A church service is no different. After a visitor comes to a service, a follow-up (email, personal note, or phone call) makes a significant impression. It is the polite thing to do, and it is the kind thing to do. For many people, that outreach may be one of the few affirmations they receive that day (or week, or ever). But let's not forget that it is also effective in building a congregation. People may enjoy the service and feel welcomed, but that post-service outreach welcoming them back is the one thing they may need to decide to return.

Exercises

1. Think about your last audience (congregation, business meeting, or event). What makes these folks tick? What do they love? What do they hate? What keeps them up at night? What makes them want to get out of bed in the morning? If you had put yourself behind the eyes of that audience before you put yourself in front, would your message have changed? How?

2. Do you greet people at the door? If not, why not? How might that change people's impression or experience?

3. Do you use a manuscript for your speaking? If so, does your audience *feel* like you use a manuscript? What three things can you do to change that?

4. Use your EKG test to ask these additional questions: Can people hear clearly? Do you use the mic effectively? Do you speak at a speed that is understandable? Do you use callbacks and repetition? Do you give your audience time to enjoy the laugh, or do you step on your hold?

5. Think about a time when something unexpected happened in your service. Did you react or comment? If not, why?

6. Do you prepare special food for your guests? Or is it the standard cornbread and buttermilk leftovers?

7. Do you follow up with visitors? How? Is there a way to make their visit more intimate, more personal?

Chapter 8

Thou Shalt Not Be Exhausted by the Sabbath

Almost everything will work again if you unplug it for a few minutes.

—Anne Lamott

Question: what is one of life's great blessings that can also kill you?

Fried foods. Check.

A pet viper. Check.

Weekly preaching. Check.

Wait, *what?*

Oh, yes. Weekly preaching is one of life's great blessings that also has the potential to kill you. I've seen it in the pulpit and I've seen it in comedy.

One of the hardest things as a new stand-up is the incessant grind of open mics. You have to pay your dues. You have to get on stage behind that mic, plowing through your set, over and over. Night after night. And if you don't pace yourself, you'll never make it for the long haul. Comedy is not funny when performed from a stretcher. Nor is preaching joyous when performed from a place of pain and exhaustion.

To be fair, there are a few preliminary things that need to be said to balance out my harsh truth. Being asked to offer a sermon to a community of faith is one of life's greatest honors. We are taken into people's trust, invited to offer nourishment for their mental and spiritual health, offered valuable time on their Sunday morning when many would prefer to be home getting a few extra hours of sleep before the blitz of the workweek begins.

It is also a great gift for the preacher (when you have the peace of mind to see it). It disciplines us into a weekly routine of study and theological wrestling. It encourages us to keep a close watch on the intersection of Scripture, the weekly headlines, and what is happening in our pews. And it allows a platform for our own hearts to speak a truth that may well find its way into other people's hearts and lives.

However, it's hard. Really hard. Week after week. Month after month. Year after year. It's the same pattern. You finish the sermon on Sunday, go to coffee hour, then head home and collapse into a coma-like nap. After thirty minutes (or hours, depending on your level of exhaustion), you open your eyes and the first thought in your mind is . . . what am I going to preach next Sunday? A friend of mine who is a spiritual director once called it "the relentless onslaught of the Sabbath."

We all feel something like this once in a while (or daily). Even if you love preaching. Even if you are brand new and have only been preaching for a few years. Even if you are the most pious lover of the liturgical calendar known to humanity. It doesn't matter. Consistent weekly preaching can wear-you-down. Studies have shown that members of the clergy suffer from high rates of physical and emotional distress, such as depression and burnout. But we know it because we live it.

Why am I talking about this? Because our physical and mental health affects our preaching. Here's an analogy. I like cooking with cast iron. At least I did until I once tried to cook breakfast in my favorite cast-iron skillet the day after I cooked a piece of salmon in it. Little did I know that fish oils seep into cast iron and flavor your future dishes. Not so good with pancakes.

Over the years, I have found that giving a sermon or a talk is similar. We are the cast iron. If we allow a smelly, unpleasant experience to permeate our surface, our entire message will be flavored by it. It could be anything from feeling physical pain to dealing with a relationship issue to worrying about a conflict with someone in the congregation. Whatever it is, if allowed to sink in, the power of the message can be gutted by the messenger.

How to Avoid the Sabbath Slump

Let us run with endurance the race set out for us.

—Hebrews 12:1

There are seven trillion clergy self-care books on Amazon. You can read all of those, or you can try the five things I've suggested below. (My list is shorter.)

Eat and Run

Lower your expectations and claim a victory.

—Rev. Andrew Mullin

The year before seminary, I decided to take a road trip from New York to Alaska and back. Not having a lot of money, I bought cheap gas and ate McDonald's every day. All was fine until I hit the Canadian Rockies and my Jeep started sputtering and my clothes got tight.

I was wearing overalls.

You get the picture.

Whether you're on a cross-country drive or involved in a weekly preaching schedule, you have to take care of yourself for the long haul. That includes feeding yourself well.

Stand-up comedians and preachers have many things in common, but one that is near and dear to my heart is our diets. In both professions, it is common to eat poorly, drink a few too many festive beverages, and generally not take care of ourselves. Part of it is stress, part of it is counteracting depression and anxiety, and part of it is that it just tastes good. Given the demands of the preaching life and the life of a stand-up, it is easy to drop into a pattern of using dry Cabernet and a medium-rare cheeseburger with truffle fries and a side of mayo as a way to get through. (If that sounds suspiciously specific, it is. Yes, I have. Let's move on.)

It's a vicious cycle. We don't eat right, and God forbid we darken the door of a gym. Which means our bodies start to feel it and show it. Then our self-image plummets (and this, as we know, affects our preaching). Which means we return to self-medicating through Cabernet and burgers. And while a dry Cab and a medium-rare burger feel great at the time, over time they will cut your stamina short. There are two easy ways to break this cycle. Ironically, they are the same two things that I was always taught were impolite: eat and run.

One of the oldest people on record was Emma Morano, who lived to be 117 years and 137 days. When asked about her secret to longevity, she replied, "Three raw eggs a day and staying single." While I wouldn't necessarily suggest her diet (or her relationship advice), I like her attitude. But, there are easier ways to eat for longevity.

For example, start with a decent breakfast. Especially before a worship service! A personal word of warning from experience: Cap'n Crunch will wear off sometime near the first minute and a half of a sermon. Eat something that will slow burn through the service. Like Emma Morano's eggs (but cook 'em). As the week goes on, throw in some salads along the way. (FYI: You can add bacon to salad and it's still a salad.) In the end, enjoy your cheeseburgers and Cabernet—life's short. But keep it in check.

I said there were two steps: eat *and* run. And no, I don't mean you have to go out and buy a $150.00 pair of New Balance shoes and start training for a marathon. You just gotta move. This could mean anything from a twenty-minute walk to something more challenging. When we move, not only are our creative juices stirred, but the body also releases a blast of endorphins, a natural painkiller that also causes a mild euphoria—a natural high. A twenty-minute walk, and voilà, you feel better, start to look better, feel less driven to self-medicate. We're in this for the long haul, and we need to eat and run to get us to the mountaintop.

Shabbat? Why Not!

If you win the rat race, you're still a rat in first place.

—Anonymous

Creative types, including preachers, stand-ups, and writers, have to have breaks for mental recovery and wellness. I am rolling my eyes as I write this because I know how clichéd that sounds. For one thing, Western society teaches us the opposite. We are what we produce. We don't need rest! Rest is for sissies. We have thirty-seven more goals for our day. And we're only on number 3.

But I return to my original statement: we need breaks for mental recovery and wellness. Fast is not necessarily good. As the old saying goes, the number on the speedometer isn't always an indication of how fast you're getting to where you're going; you could be going in circles. Taking a break is the only way you'll figure out your trajectory.

One of my best life lessons came from a tiny silver-haired woman with a twinkle in her eye. I met Nana Gert, the grandmother of a dear friend, many years ago when I first moved from North Carolina to New York. Upon hearing that I was new in town and had no family in the area, Nana Gert insisted on inviting me, a Baptist from the South, to her famous Shabbat dinners on Long Island.

Each week, I would gather with her family around her table, which simply groaned under the weight of matzo ball soup, veal cutlets, and noodle kugel. Marveling at how Nana Gert, who was in her mid-eighties, had the energy to prepare such a huge dinner every week, I finally asked her for her secret. She explained it like this: "Traditionally, Jews celebrate Shabbat on Friday evenings into Saturday. But at my age, I need a break—a Shabbat—more than once a week! So, whenever I'm tired, whether it be on a Friday or a Monday or a Wednesday, I sit down, and declare, 'Shabbat? Why not!'"

I have always tried to follow Nana Gert's wisdom by declaring when I'm tired, "Shabbat? Why not!" It is not admirable, or inspiring to your congregation, for you to work nonstop. We must mirror Sabbath to them like any other scriptural teaching. Working nonstop also makes for some piss-poor sermons (and comedy routines).

Avoiding this could mean something as simple as saying, "No." Author Tim Ferris suggests having a "Not-to-do List," containing things like *not* checking email constantly, *not* agreeing to meetings with no agenda or clear end time, and, my personal favorite, not expecting work to fill a void that non-work relationships and activities should fill. In the end, when you say yes to something, it's imperative that you understand what you're saying no to.

"Shabbat? Why not!" also means take your vacation time: daily, weekly, monthly, quarterly, yearly vacations. A daily vacation might be a brief nap. Studies show that a quick shut-eye (twenty to thirty minutes) can stop deterioration in performance, and an hour-long nap can even reverse it. If not a nap, then take five minutes to breathe. There are multiple apps and videos that offer guided meditations or breathing exercises.

Your monthly vacation might be a nice dinner or a day trip away somewhere new. Quarterly, take a weekend away that involves a Sunday. Yearly, take a proper vacation and get out of town to a place you love for at least two weeks. If getting out of town is not an option, take a "staycation" (meaning stay home but stay away from the church) and explore new things in your town that you never have a chance to enjoy.

I also highly encourage you to take sabbaticals. Many denominations offer it as a matter of policy every five to ten years. It is the best thing imaginable not only for a pastor but also for the congregation. They need a break, too. They need to know they can exist without you. But most important, they need to know they miss you and need you back.

Pray

I give God the first hour of my day, and God gives me the rest.

—Dr. Martin Luther King, Jr.

I once heard a man who was training for a marathon say something to the effect of "If I can complete this race, I will be a better person."

Hmm.

I'm all for self-improvement, but "better person"? That statement made me realize how many things we do in an endless gerbil-wheel effort to make ourselves worthy, better, lovable.

Running a marathon won't save you. Nor will preaching a great sermon. Or having a packed-to-overflowing church. Or winning the Powerball jackpot. (Although, I'd be willing to roll the dice on the latter just to see.) What you are—right now—is enough.

In Matthew 3:17, God said to Jesus, "You are my beloved in whom I am well pleased." The most striking thing? God said these words before Jesus picked any disciples, preached one sermon, worked any miracles, raised any dead people, healed any blind people, or slapped down any demons. Interesting timing. God offers Jesus these words before he has *done* anything. It's like God was saying it is enough. *You* are enough.

God doesn't need us to run ourselves onto a stretcher to be loved. It doesn't work like that. If we think that's true, then that's *our* issue, culled from years of family baggage and life experiences, not God's. And tragically, we adopt these crazy, self-imposed standards as things we must achieve in order to be worthy. Chasing impossible standards leads to self-criticism (internal hecklers), which leads to decreased productivity, which leads to more criticism, which eventually leads to chronic illness.

Now don't get all New Age/self-help on me. I'm not saying don't challenge yourself. I'm not saying don't have dreams. I'm saying wake up and reach for the stars, but at the end of the day, rejoice in what you got done and then stop, say a prayer, and know in your deepest heart, "I am loved, and it is enough."

The irony is that we, as pastors, sometimes let this most powerful source of healing slip. We preach about the power of prayer all the time, but the reality is that most of us have numerous board meetings, multiple people who need pastoral visits, a roof that is falling in, and, as always, a sermon bearing down. No pastor wants to admit that their dedication to their prayer life has slid to the level of their dedication to reading denominational newsletters.

But it does.

Gandhi said prayer was "the key of the morning and the bolt of the evening." We need to train ourselves to tap the power of prayer every day.

Laugh

Eat half, walk double, laugh triple, and love without measure.

—Tibetan proverb

One thing that comedians have going for them in stressful times is laughter. That's our job. That's what we do. So we are constantly thinking up funny things and trying them out on each other. Which means we're laughing. A lot.

Unfortunately, pastors don't generally laugh like that. We have to go out of our way to remind ourselves to laugh. But there are powerful reasons to do so.

First, laughter makes the day better. I once heard someone say, "If you've laughed and created, it's a good day." Amen. To laugh with someone, or by yourself, lifts up your heart and elevates your spirit. Celebrate something every day. And if you're not sure what to celebrate, check out this resource that gives celebrations for every day of the year.

Second, laughter helps keep things in perspective. As I said in *Laugh Your Way to Grace,* "If you can laugh at yourself, you can forgive yourself. And if you can forgive yourself, you can forgive others."

Third, laughter brings physical and spiritual healing. The extra air intake from laughter lowers blood pressure, improves heart and lung function, and increases endorphins. It also can be argued that it brings us closer to God. The theologian Karl Barth said, "Laughter is the closest thing to the grace of God." While Karl and I are on very different theological planes, I do think he's onto something here. The Hebrew word for breath, *ruach,* is also the same word for spirit. As we laugh, we breathe in air *and* spirit. You might even say that as we laugh, we inhale and exhale the power of God.

Humor is also critical during times of crisis. I'm a breast cancer survivor, and humor is the thing that got me through. It reminded me that my pain was only something I was experiencing, not who I was. To laugh in a place of pain reminds us that we still have hope.

(In the appendix, I have listed many organizations dedicated to using humor to heal.)

How do we as pastors remember to laugh? I keep a collection of irreverent religious tchotchkes (Yiddish for "miscellaneous random junk") in my office that makes me laugh every time I see it. Stuff like the sign on my desk that says, "Not Today Satan!" or a nun robot that when wound up spits fire. My rubber duck nativity scene makes me smile. So does the brewery T-shirt from Salt Lake City that advertises a local beer called "Polygamy Porter" with a tag line that says, "Why have just one?" My all-time favorite, however, is Pink Jesus, a pink plastic statue of Jesus with a magic eight ball in his feet that answers your every question.

You can also access a multitude of things online to make you laugh, like "Pachelbel's Chicken" where a young man plays the entire classical "Pachelbel's Canon" with rubber chickens. This link is worth the entire price of the book.

If that's not enough, how about virtual bubble wrap where you can sit at your computer and pop bubbles to your heart's content?

Or you can enjoy anything that comedian John Crist has created. Try this video titled "If Bible Characters Had iPhones."

We must remember to laugh. It may well be God's greatest gift.

Remember Why You Do What You Do

A vision without a task is but a dream, a task without a vision is drudgery, a vision with a task is the hope of the world.

—Church inscription, Sussex, England (1730)

We have to remember to laugh, and, equally important, we must take time to remember why we do what we do. Why do we get up and preach? Sure, it's our job. But what's the real reason?

When I lose track, I take a break and return to a memory from my early childhood. It involved Saturday nights when I would pile my stuffed animals in the corner of my room and make up sermons for them. I loved doing it, and I knew that my sermon would be way better than that of the Gandalf from Lord of the Rings–lookin' preacher the next morning. While the Southern Baptist Church shut down my dream of preaching early on, it came back for me later in life with a vengeance. Now I channel the dream of that little six-year-old every Sunday.

What was your moment of knowing being a pastor was your call? Your dream? Take a break, be kind to yourself, and remember why you do what you do. And if you can't, if the dream or call has faded or is not what it used to be, you need to be aware of that, too.[1] God's call is not static, nor is it a one-time thing. It is an ongoing conversation to which we must stay carefully attuned. As someone who did a hairpin turn in the middle of her career, I can say with some credibility that there is no shame in changing jobs or even careers—only in staying in a place where your heart no longer resides.

Exercises

1. Does your diet (physical and spiritual) support the long haul?

2. When was your last vacation? If it was long ago, why?

3. Are you due a sabbatical? What opportunities are there in your community or denomination that would support such a respite?

4. What makes you laugh? What can you put in your office that will remind you to laugh (and invite others to laugh as well)?

5. Why do you do what you do? Is your heart still in it?

---

1. See Taylor, *Leaving Church*.

Chapter 9

Thou Shalt Achieve World Peace through Humor

Physicians, psychologists and psychiatrists believe that humor helps in the healing process of the physical body. If we take seriously the Pauline image of the body of Christ, we might ask if the same holds true for the Christian community. In the midst of some of the worst times in the church, the people of God could sure use some laughter.

—Fr. James Martin, editor, *America Magazine*

Comedians have long known a secret that world and religious leaders are still struggling to understand to this day: humor is the key to world peace. Why it's so complicated, I have no idea. Perhaps it's because we've tended to dismiss the true power of humor and laughter. I'll never forget a professor who once told me that my dream of being a theologian and a comedian was "cute but had no place in serious study." As my Southern mother used to say when she thought something was suspect, "Well" (pronounced with several syllables and a skeptical lilt).

Well.

Don't mind me. I'm just going to take my cute comedy and save the world. And here are the five ways I'm going do it:

Start with What We Have in Common

Love your crooked neighbor with your own crooked heart.

—W. H. Auden, poet

One of science's greatest achievements is the mapping of the human gene, and the results are startling: notwithstanding race, ethnicity, gender, or nationality, human beings are 99.99 percent the same.

I'll give you a moment to let that sink in.

The upshot of this is that all our human conflicts, violence, and even warfare are over 0.01 percent. It's hard to believe that we are killing each other over such a teeny, tiny difference. Yet we can't forgive that difference. In his book *The Wise Heart*, author Jack Kornfield tells a story of two POWs. One says to the other, "Have you forgiven your captors yet?" The second man thinks for a moment and then says, "No, never." The other one responded, "Well then, they still have you in prison."

Humor is the one thing that can help us let go of that inability to forgive because it highlights our commonalities. When we laugh with someone, whether it is a stranger, a friend, or an enemy, our worlds overlap for a tiny but significant moment. If we both react to a joke, it means we share an experience that allows us both to understand the punchline. It is then that our differences fade and our common connections gleam forth.

Talk about the Hard Stuff

A spoon full of sugar makes the medicine go down.

—Mary Poppins

Years ago, I owned a black Labrador retriever named Stuart. I adored Stuart and because of that he was a bit . . . let's say, privileged. For example, he loved bacon. And who doesn't? I used it for treats, for a bedtime snack, and, most important, for getting him to take medicine.

Stuart would not under any circumstances ingest a pill. But if it were wrapped in a piece of bacon, he would swallow it before you could blink. What he tasted up front was the delicious bacon, but as the morsel started being digested, the healing element would slowly begin to be absorbed. And that is one of the most powerful things about humor: it takes difficult topics, wraps them in metaphorical bacon, and then allows the medicine, the difficult conversations, to begin working.

I was in New York City on September 11, 2001, when terrorists flew planes into the World Trade Center towers and the Pentagon. It was not a time for laughing. Nor was it a time when any comedians dared get on stage. Except one. In the weeks following 9/11, the stand-up comedian Reno bravely opened a comedy show off-Broadway. The show, *Rebel without a Pause*, was framed around her experiences on that dreadful day. Heralded as an instant hit, her comedy provided a safe space for the audience to simultaneously experience their grief as well as laugh at their common experiences. Noting the designer luggage carried by her escaping neighbors in the exclusive Tribeca community, and their clear status as "first-time runners," Reno dubbed them "nouvelle refugees from Tribecastan." She went on to inquire, "Where was the emergency broadcast system that day?" and "Why was the National Guard wearing *jungle* camouflage in Manhattan?" Her material walked us, the audience, many of whom had lost loved ones in the attack, through the trauma of 9/11, evoking laughter, then tears, then more laughter, and finally hope.

It's true for difficult situations, and it's true for difficult sermons. Pastors have a responsibility to talk about the hard stuff—to call out the rampant injustice we see in our world. As Rev. Dr. William J. Barber II said, "Cute, cuddly preaching that does not trouble or take the risk of the gospel is theological malpractice at best, heresy at worst."[1]

We don't usually think of humor as a tool in presenting difficult topics like racism or bigotry. However, sometimes humor can be the way in; it can establish trust and rapport, which then allow us to

---

1. Barber's foreword to Taylor, *How to Preach a Dangerous Sermon*, Kindle loc. 235.

preach truth to power. Take a moment and check out my sermon "It's Our Time to Move." There, I use the "Standstill Parade" (from chapter 2) as a humorous entrée to a fierce sermon on racism.

Defuse Conflict

If I can't dance . . . then it ain't my revolution.

—Emma Goldman, political activist and writer

When I think about the power of humor to defuse conflict, I think of Jesus' teaching to turn the other cheek. For some, that story sounds passive. But look at it from a martial arts perspective: if someone hits you and you turn the other cheek, you not only miss the backhand blow, the more powerful of the two, but also throw your enemy off-balance. Said another way, you use your opponent's energy without giving yours away.

Years back when I was practicing law, the phone rang one January morning in my Long Island City, New York, office. Even before I said hello, a voice started screaming at me on the other line about how my client was going to get sued for millions of dollars. I placed the call on speakerphone as the rant from the plaintiff's lawyer continued, and I flipped through my inbox to find the papers. After a moment, I saw it: a draft complaint with the heading "In the Circuit Court of Oahu, State of Hawaii."

I immediately picked up the receiver.

"Please sue me as soon as possible. I'll give you my home address if that helps. I'll even pay the Federal Express costs to serve the complaint."

Long pause. "Are you crazy?" he asked.

"Nope. For your information, I'm located in Long Island City, which is basically a burned-out warehouse district in Queens, New York. It is gray, sleeting, and it is 13 degrees. You are threatening to sue me in Oahu. So, I say again, sue me now!"

After another pause, a muffled laugh came through the receiver. We ended up chatting about the outrageous difference in our weather that morning and the fact that we both hated cold. I shared that

I had an aunt who had visited Hawaii, and he related that he had relatives who live in the Bronx. After a few moments of pleasantries and finding common ground, we turned to the case and within ten minutes had agreed on an equitable resolution.

The ability to laugh in that moment was like letting off steam from a pressure cooker. When we laughed, it broke the tension. And in that moment of truce, we were able to communicate without anger and find a solution.

St. Francis described it like this: "Let me not seek as much . . . to be understood as to understand." Conflict resolution experts call this interest-based negotiation, meaning that you focus on why the issue is important to the other side rather than the rightness or wrongness of your respective positions. By identifying shared values, you find common ground, and it is from that place of commonality that solutions more easily flow. And what is the quickest way to find a shared value? Humor.

Speaking Truth to Power

It [humor] plays close to the big hot fire which is Truth, and sometimes the reader feels the heat.

—E. B. White

Most people are familiar with the Danish folktale by Hans Christian Andersen titled "The Emperor's New Clothes." It is about an emperor who hires two tailors who promise to make him a set of remarkable new clothes that will be invisible to anyone who is either incompetent or stupid. In reality, the tailors don't make any clothes, and the emperor parades around naked. Everyone in the kingdom pretends to see the clothes until a child finally yells out, "He hasn't got any clothes on!"

Power is threatened by humor because, like Andersen's folktale, it calls out reality, it shows things for what they are, and it levels the playing field. A great example was seen in 2007 when the Ku Klux Klan had planned a march in downtown Knoxville to proclaim their hate-filled message of "white power." Locals decided to meet that hatred with humor, organizing a counter-protest with a gathering of clowns (or, as the troupe was called, the "Coup Clutz Clowns").

The clowns did things like pretending not to understand the shouts of "White power!" "White flour?" they yelled, and threw white baking flour in the air, all over the street and the Klan marchers. Some yelled, "Tight shower?" and sprayed the crowd from a showerhead. Other clowns wore wedding dresses and yelled "Wife power!" dancing behind the Klan. Eventually, the Klan, gutted of dignity and any sense of power, dispersed and went home.[2]

Another example of humor threatening power was seen during 2014 in a small village in Germany. The town's residents had grown tired of the neo-Nazis marching in their square. So, for every meter the group progressed during the next march, the town donated 10 euros to an organization that helped people leave right-wing extremist groups. Residents threw confetti at the end of the parade to celebrate the fact that the neo-Nazis had raised 12,000 euros against their own cause.

When speaking truth to power, it helps to include a humorous twist. This tactic tends to throw power off its game.

Building Bridges

Days pass, and the years vanish, and we walk sightless among miracles.

—Jewish Sabbath prayer

One of my greatest joys is being part of the Laugh in Peace comedy tour, which stars three comics: a Baptist (me), a rabbi, and a Muslim (the scariest of the three, of course, being the Baptist).

In the show, Rabbi Bob Alper tells about studying in Israel during seminary. Anxious to try out his biblical Hebrew, he told his cab driver—in Hebrew—to let him out. The driver burst out laughing, explaining that Bob had literally said, "BEHOLD! Here I descend!"

---

2. This story was memorialized in *White Flour* by David LaMotte.

I talk about the often-limited worldview of Christians, especially my people, the Baptists: "Southern Baptists, for example, can toe a hard line. At least their theology is short and sweet. Like their idea of heaven: 'You ain't Southern Baptist? You ain't coming.' That's like 6.5 billion people not coming. If you look at a world map, that's every landmass on the face of the globe . . . except Texas and Alabama."

Our Muslim comic Azhar Usman has a riff on what it's like being Muslim in America, especially in airports. He says, "I don't get why you guys are so upset about having to be at the airport two hours before your flights. I have to be there *two months* ahead."

Our audiences, wearing everything from yarmulkes and burkas to Easter hats, walk away with a rare visual: Jewish, Christian, and Muslim together—not hating, not judging, but laughing in solidarity. It's in that laughter that our worlds (ours and the audiences') overlap for a tiny but significant moment and we lock into our common humanity.

One of the questions we get in our Q & A after the show is, "How far can you go with comedy before it crosses a line or becomes disrespectful?" All comedians have their own rules about what is appropriate comedic material. For me, it's simple. I imagine a circle around my feet. Anything within that circle, meaning anything that I represent, is fair game. That means I can craft comedy about women, ministers, lawyers, redheads, people who love onion dip, Southerners, Baptists, New Yorkers who aren't from New York, and on and on. The moment I go outside that circle is when I risk transforming humor from healing to divisive.

Why risk it? The healing power of humor is too strong. A great example of this happened at one of our Laugh in Peace college shows. The event was sponsored by the local Jewish student group and the Muslim student group. Backstage before the event, the presidents of each organization were overheard busily deciding where they were going to eat together after the show. Later, they told us that even though their offices were right next to one another in the student union, before they began working on Laugh in Peace, they'd never spoken to each other. And now they were friends—hanging out. Bottom line: If you laugh together, you can't hate each other.

You just can't.

Are we going to achieve world peace through humor overnight? No. But it will start a ripple effect that will change how we see each other and, eventually, change the world.

Exercises

1. How can you use humor to highlight what people in your congregation have in common with those who are different from them?

2. How have you seen humor used to speak truth to power? Was it effective? Why or why not?

3. Is there tension in your community or your family that could be eased with humor?

4. Consider connecting with a different community of faith, preferably one of a different belief, and sharing food and laughter. Then watch and see what happens.

Chapter 10

Thou Shalt Have Joyous Communication

It's showtime, folks!

—Joe Gideon, *All That Jazz*

You may remember the above quote from the 1979 movie *All That Jazz*. The line spoken by Joe Gideon, played by Roy Scheider, a chain-smoking, pill-popping choreographer-director by day and playboy by night. Every morning he greets his hungover, bloodshot image in the bathroom mirror with, "It's showtime, folks!"

While hopefully you aren't feeling like Joe Gideon, we all face personal issues that we have to negotiate as we stand behind our pulpits and podiums. We all have those pre-sermon moments when the hecklers in our heads are screaming. And at some point, we will all find ourselves standing in front of our congregation after a horrendous tragedy in our community, nation, or world, thinking *how can I possibly hold this family together and offer a message of hope?*

But that's what's required of a preacher: to stand firm in the face of this broken world, transcending our own individual pain, self-doubts, and fears, offering a message of hope. My friend and mentor Rev. Dr. Otis Moss III called it "Preaching about tragedy but refusing to fall into despair."[1] In the end, no matter what's going on, we have to find the strength to look back in the mirror and say, "It's showtime."[2]

The best advice I've ever gotten on this issue was from my comedy coach. He taught us that, five minutes before getting up to perform our set, we should put down our notes and remind ourselves that there is nowhere else we would rather be than that dark, smoky comedy club, and nothing more exciting than the material we have to share. That joy will radiate out to the audience, and the audience, in turn, will respond.

He calls it "joyous communication." And for him that is the ballgame.

> If the audience picks up from you that there is nowhere else on earth you'd rather be than onstage talking to them, then they start thinking, *I'm having a ball here, listening to this guy [or gal].* If, however, you go onstage thinking . . . *let me get this over with*, then your audience will start thinking GET THIS OVER WITH.

He goes on to explain that "[w]hen individuals become an audience, a transformation takes place. They stop feeling what each of them is feeling individually, and they start to feel collectively what the performer is feeling."[3]

I believe the same is true for all communicators, especially preachers and religious leaders. No matter how we feel, we must radiate joyous communication into the rafters and far corners of the sanctuary. We have to show up every time with the fullest sense of joy we can muster. Why? Because what we bring into the pulpit, the congregation takes away.

---

1 Moss, *Blue Note Preaching in a Post-Soul World*, 6.

2. OK, I know that some of you may be offended by my using the term "show" for a worship service. Feel free. But from the perspective of a modest parish pastor without a seventeen-person worship/tech/light/sound team (i.e., me), running a worship service can easily feel like you are the producer, the director, and the master of ceremonies.

3. Rosenfield, *Mastering Stand-up*, 9.

Joy Is Contagious

If you bring forth what is within you, it will save you; if you do not bring forth what is within you, it will destroy you.

—Gospel of Thomas

Psychologists and scientists as far back as Charles Darwin have argued that emotions can be regulated by behavior. We usually think the opposite—that we smile when we are feeling happy. But science has shown that we can create happiness by the act of forming a smile.

For example, there is scientific evidence to show that when a person smiles, it triggers physiological changes in the brain that cool the blood, which in turn controls our mood, which in the end causes a feeling of happiness. Translated: we can change our inward emotion by changing our outward expression.

I've said that what we feel in our hearts manifests itself in our behavior, and how we act over time is what we become. Consistently reminding ourselves to smile throughout our daily lives may eventually change our hearts. And when our hearts change, the way we encounter the world changes. That is when we can truly begin to affect those around us.

I think of the famous lyrics by Louis Armstrong: "When you're smiling, the whole world smiles with you." Louis was onto something, as science has proven those lyrics to be true. Neuroscience has shown that merely seeing a smile (or a frown) activates mirror neurons in the brain that mimic the emotion. Translated: When someone smiles at us, we smile back. And vice versa.

This research has caught on in a number of industries, including the hospitality industry. For example, Walt Disney World as well as the Ritz Carlton use what's called the 10:5 Rule. When a hotel employee is within ten feet of a guest, they must make eye contact and smile. When they get within five feet of the guest, they must say hello. Bottom line? Joy is contagious.

Tap the Source

Ain't nobody, nowhere, nothin' without God.

—Duke Ellington

I said in the introduction that the message we preach is "good news." It is about joy. In fact, the word "joy" appears in the Bible more than 160 times—more than the words "hell" and "hate" combined. No where do you see the spirit of joy more clearly than in Psalms:

- "He will make me smile again for he is my God!" (Ps 43:5)
- "I am radiant with joy because of your mercy, for you have listened to my troubles and have seen the crisis in my soul." (Ps 31: 7)
- "This is the day that the LORD has made. We will rejoice and be glad in it." (Ps 188:24)
- "All who seek for God shall live in joy." (Ps 69:32)

If you want to go New Testament, there's the announcement at Jesus' birth: "And the angel said unto them, Fear not: for, behold, I bring you good tidings of great joy, which shall be to all people" (Luke 2:10). Or Jesus' words in the book of John: "I have said these things to you so that my joy may be in you, and that your joy may be complete" (John 15:11).

Perhaps the most powerful statement of the organic nature of God's joy is from Isaiah:

> The Spirit of the Sovereign LORD is on me, because the LORD has anointed me to proclaim good news to the poor. He has sent me to bind up the brokenhearted, to proclaim freedom for the captives and release from darkness for the prisoners . . . and provide for those who grieve in Zion—to bestow on them a crown of beauty instead of ashes, the oil of joy instead of mourning. (Isa 61:1-3)

It's a message of joy! So why not tap the source?

Think of Thomas Edison. He never questioned the existence of electricity. He always believed that if the power didn't work, it wasn't the power; it was a problem with the *transmission* of the power.

God is the power source. If we don't feel the power, it's not God; it's a problem with our transmission. There's a saying that goes, "If God seems silent, who moved?" We can choose to plug into this ultimate life force, or we can choose to plug into the things of the world that offer no ultimate power and therefore leave us flat and dim.

Here's the honest truth: Preaching without a holy connection is just a motivational speech. There's nothing wrong with motivational speaking. I do it for a living. But it's not a sermon.

A sermon is bigger than us. In its purest form, a sermon should be a message inspired from a higher power given through you to a congregation. You are the medium. You can connect to the source and radiate that message with fire, power, joy, and light.

Or you can reduce it to a speech.

Your call.

For me, tapping that power week after week requires a group effort. In addition to the obvious collaboration with the Lord, it involves me, author Julia Cameron, a fake fireplace, Fred Craddock, fabulous cowboy boots, and Anne Lamott. The first stop is Julia. I love her book *The Artist's Way*, especially her morning pages exercises. There, you spend ten minutes writing down all the crazy stuff in your head at the moment—all the "I wish I hadn'ts" or "Oh, I haven't done this and that." No stopping, no pausing. Total stream of consciousness. The purpose is to clear out all the trash and baggage that block our ability to hear the creative divine voice.

Once there is some space between my ears, I set a timer for another ten minutes, sit by my fake fireplace, and simply breathe and wait.[4] Some would call that meditation. I think of it as inviting, even summoning, the Spirit. When the timer goes off, I start to write.

I repeat these steps (Julie, fire, write) every weekday morning. Once the sermon is close to finished (which, for me, takes most of

---

4. We all have to find the things that make our hearts happy. I love a crackling wood fire. But since my church office is in midtown Manhattan, that ain't happening. So, I bought a fake fireplace from Home Depot with aluminum-foil flames and a remote control. It's on every day—winter, spring, summer, fall.

the week), that's when Fred Craddock comes in. He suggests praying the sermon—literally.

He explains that you should begin by saying, "Gracious God," and then start reading your sermon. As he says, "Pray it. It's amazing how that will bleed out all the . . . small-minded things. You're suddenly made to realize that the primary audience of this sermon is God."[5] I find that to be a powerful exercise not only in reframing the focus on God but also in editing. Reading a sermon, essay, speech, or book out loud is the quickest way to see the editorial problems.

Finally, Sunday morning, right before I start the service, I slip into some fabulous cowboy boots (to help me kick some homiletic butt), and then I raise up Anne Lamott's three-word prayer (now a book): *Thanks, Help, Wow.* Between the preparation steps, the boots, and that three-word prayer, I am reminded to be grateful for the opportunity of the day, reminded that I can't do this alone, and, most important, reminded of the joy and the miracle of every moment.

What It Could Be

If there is a disease in the preaching that I hear most often, it's not that what the minister says is wrong. It's that it is just too small.

—Fred Craddock

If the goal in a comedy club is laughter, then the goal in a pulpit is joy. Sure, there are days when the "joy" must be tempered with a call to justice or a somber message of comfort during times of crisis. But in the end, we must leave our congregations with a sense of joy. Because with joy comes hope, and with hope comes love, and that's the best we can do as preachers and as human beings.

I remind myself of that every few months when I visit the Astor Place Kmart on the Lower East Side of Manhattan. Specifically, I favor an area in the far back corner of the basement. It is devoid of windows or natural light, with a back wall of clear glass that faces the

5. Overdorf, *One Year to Better Preaching*, 266.

dungeon-like dark tunnel of the Number 6 subway train. There, you will find the most unexpected thing: a plant nursery.

Sprouting out of this dreary prison are tender green leaves of ficus trees and the vibrant gold blossoms of marigolds. I rescue a few, bringing them back to my home to die in peace. But still, I hold out hope for them, thanks to the tiny plastic tab peeking out of each pot with an image of what that particular plant *could* grow into if it received proper light and care.

I'm inspired by their fight. Even amid the bleak circumstances, these tiny plants still struggle, every moment of every day, to tap into the energy around them (bleak as it is) so that they might grow into their potential.

So, too, we may not always be surrounded with the light and air that we need, but we still have the opportunity to grow into our potential—to lift people up, to lighten their load, and to change their reality. We have the gift of being able to make a difference in people's lives through our works and through our words. As the Benedictine nun Joan Chittister so beautifully explained, "We have the potential to be the human beat of the heart of God."

And like those little plants, we have to fight for it. So we climb onto our ramparts Sunday after Sunday, holding our ground to the last second as we share our joy. Then we climb down. Go home. Take a nap. Enjoy time with people we love and call it a well-lived day. Because tomorrow will dawn and we'll eat a decent breakfast, take an EKG test from our last sermon, learn, think, breathe, and start again.

We have to start again. Because what we do matters. The world is starving for joy. And when offered, our healing, our grace, our words, and our joy will be felt in deeper and broader places than we could ever imagine.

But time is ticking. There's not one moment to waste. As the words from the Jewish Talmud warn, "when we are called to our maker, we will each be held responsible for all the opportunities for joy that we ignored."

Brothers and sisters, we are the recipients of a great gift of joy—a gift, which if allowed, can heal the most broken of places. Let's honor this gift (and the giver). Let's commit to lifting up one heart at a time. Let's pledge that we will spend our days filling the world with joy and hope. And let's do it—together—through preaching punchlines.

Exercises

1. How do you communicate with joy when you are in a place of pain? How do you preach about tragedy without falling into despair?

2. When was the last time you used a smile to change someone's expression? To change the mood of a meeting? To change the tenor of a room?

3. How do you tap the power source? Have you ever delivered a motivational speech instead of a sermon?

4. If God gave you a plastic tab with an image of what you could grow into, what would it look like?

5. What are the opportunities for joy that you have ignored? Are you ready to now take advantage?

Appendix

Join our *Preaching Punchlines* community! Scan the code (or visit www.susansparks.com/online-courses/) to access free resources, connect with our Facebook group, and check out our online course!

Organizations that Use Humor to Heal

Association of Applied and Therapeutic Humor
www.aath.org

Comedy Cures
www.ComedyCures.org

Clowns without Borders
www.clownswithoutborders.org

Pediatric Hospital Clowns
www.healthyhumorinc.org

Patch Adams and the Gesundheit Institute
www.patchadams.org

Stand-up as Treatment for Mental Health Issues
www.standupformentalhealth.com/

Laughter Yoga
www.laughteryoga.org

Laughter on Call (using humor to combat dementia)
https://laughteroncall.com

Mad Libs Scripture

A New Look at the Good Samaritan, Luke 10:30-37

And Jesus answered, saying,

A certain man went down from _____ (modern town) and fell among thieves, who stripped him of his _____ (nice item of designer clothing/jewelry) and wounded him and then departed, leaving him half dead.

And by chance there came down a certain _____ (title for a modern religious leader) that way. And when she saw him, she simply passed by on the other side.

And likewise, a _____ (high-level corporate title) came and looked on him and passed by on the other side.

But a certain _____ (a person who is disliked), as he journeyed, came where he was, and when he saw him, he had compassion on him.

And he went to him and bound up his wounds, pouring in _____ (name of a drug store first aid item), set him on his own _____ (modern mode of transportation), brought him to a _____ (name of a modern hotel), and took care of him.

And the next day when he departed, he took out _____ (method of payment), and gave it to the host, and said unto him, _____ (a modern, hip, slang greeting) take care of him; and if you spend more than I have given you, when I come again, I will repay you.

Sermon Excerpts

Excerpt from "Pass the Tabasco"

Sermon by Rev. Susan Sparks
Madison Avenue Baptist Church
May 11, 2008
Pentecost

A reading from Acts 2:1-4, NRSV (New Revised "Susan" Version):

When the day of Pentecost had come, they were all together in one place. Peter, John, James, Andrew—the whole crowd. And a meal of bread and fish was served. Looking at the plate, Peter sighed and said, "It's bread and fish everyday. Is there nothing else?" The other disciples nodded in agreement. There was a long silence, then James (who was sitting next to Peter) pulled from his tunic a small bottle of red liquid. "Hey, this should help," he whispered to Peter. "I picked this up over at the spice market. It's called Tabasco—from some foreign land called Louisiana. I think it's near Petra or Jordan or something." Peter's eyes lit up. As he handed him the bottle, James warned, "Hey, be careful, this stuff is seriously hot. The caravan leader I bought it from said he accidentally killed a camel with it."

Peter, completely ignoring the camel story and overjoyed to have anything to perk up his meal, began pouring the Tabasco all over his fish with great glee. John (who was sitting on the other side of Peter) noticed his plate and said, "Peter, dude, what is that?" Peter was like, "It's Tabasco, man. James totally hooked me up with this stuff. You gotta try it." The next thing you know, all you hear around the table from the disciples is "Pass the Tabasco!"

After they had all been served, they began to eat. Peter took the first bite, and suddenly he started breathing heavily and fanning his mouth. Then James, then John, then all the other disciples began breathing heavily and fanning their mouths . . . and together it sounded like the rush of a violent wind, and it filled the entire house where they were sitting. Divided tongues, as of fire, appeared among them, and a tongue rested on each of them. And all of them were filled with the Holy Spirit and they began to speak in other languages [add crazy noises while waving hand in front of mouth] as the Spirit gave them ability.

One-line Sermon Summary: Experiencing the Holy Spirit is like taking a big dose of Tabasco because both bring wind, fire, and power.

Excerpt from "The True Universal Health Care"

Sermon by Rev. Susan Sparks
Madison Avenue Baptist Church
October 25, 2009

The Theologian Karl Barth said you should do theology with the Bible in one hand and the newspaper in the other. If you consider the Scripture this week in light of the headlines, you had no choice but to see it through a lens of healthcare.

As Jesus and his disciples were leaving Jericho, Bartimaeus, a blind beggar, was sitting by the roadside. When he heard that it was Jesus of Nazareth, he began to shout out and say, "Jesus, Son of David, have mercy on me!"

Several of the disciples went over and said, "Be quiet and wait your turn. Can't you see there's a crowd waiting to see the Messiah?" As Bartimaeus paused in silence, he felt a clipboard being thrust into his hands.

"Now," said John, one of the bossier of the disciples, "fill out the following thirteen forms. We need name, address, social security number, next of kin, and whether you have an HMO, PPO, or POS. Please indicate whether you have additional vision and/or dental coverage, check the box on page 5 if this is a work-related injury, fill out the duplicate form if you have any secondary insurance, read and sign the privacy statement at the end, and then return it to me with your insurance card."

Bartimaeus paused. "I can't read. I'm blind."

"Well, then," said John in a huff, "give me your insurance card and we'll try to get you in the queue anyway."

Bartimaeus shook his head in shame, mumbling something under his breath.

"What did you say?" John demanded.

"I'm uninsured."

"I still can't understand you!" John hollered.

"I AM UNINSURED!" Bartimaeus finally yelled.

A gasp came from the disciples. "Uninsured!?" they said, looking at each other with disgust, and the crowd began to back away from Bartimaeus.

"Do you have cash?" John asked.

"No," said Bartimaeus.

"Do you have a credit card?"

"No."

"Do you have a job?"

"No."

"Well, then," John snapped, "you'll simply have to find another Messiah."

Bartimaeus cried out even more loudly, "Son of David, have mercy on me!"

Jesus heard the man, stopped what he was doing, and said, "Who is that? Call him here."

And they called the blind man, saying to him, "Take heart. You've apparently been pre-qualified."

Throwing off his cloak, Bartimaeus sprang up and came to Jesus. Then Jesus said to him, "What do you want me to do for you?"

Bartimaeus said to him, "My teacher, let me see again."

Jesus said to him, "Go. Your faith has made you well."

Immediately Bartimaeus regained his sight and followed Jesus. And as he left, Jesus turned to the disciples and said, "Under no circumstances is this man to be charged a co-pay."

One-line Sermon Summary: Jesus' commandments of clothe the poor, feed the hungry, and tend the sick are universal commandments.

Bibliography

Adams, Doug. *The Prostitute in the Family Tree: Discovering Humor and Irony in the Bible.* Louisville KY: Westminster John Knox Press, 1997.

Alper, Robert. *Thanks. I Needed That. And Other Stories of the Spirit.* Canton MI: Read the Spirit Books, 2013.

Buechner, Frederick. *The Gospel as Tragedy, Comedy & Fairytale.* San Francisco: HarperSanFrancisco, 1977.

Cousins, Norman. *Anatomy of an Illness.* New York: W.W. Norton & Company, 1979.

Cote, Richard G. *Holy Mirth.* Whitinsville MA: Affirmation Books, 1986.

Cox, Harvey. *The Feast of Fools: A Theological Essay on Festivity and Fantasy.* New York: Harper & Row, 1969.

Craddock, Fred B. *As One without Authority.* St. Louis MO: Chalice Press, 2001.

———. *Craddock on the Craft of Preaching.* St. Louis MO: Chalice Press, 2011.

Errett, Benjamin. *Elements of Wit: Mastering the Art of Being Interesting.* New York: Penguin, 2014.

Freud, Sigmund. *Jokes and Their Relation to the Unconscious.* New York: W.W. Norton & Company, 1960.

Hample, Stuart, and Eric Marshall. *Children's Letters to God.* New York: Workman Publishing, 1991.

Hyers, M. Conrad. *The Comic Vision and the Christian Faith: A Celebration of Life and Laughter.* Eugene OR: Wipf & Stock, 1981.

———. *Holy Laughter: Essays on Religion in the Comic Perspective.* New York: The Seabury Press, 1969.

LaMotte, David. *White Flour.* Montreat NC: Lower Dryad Music, 2012.

Lipman, Steve. *Laughter in Hell: The Use of Humor during the Holocaust.* Northvale NJ: Jason Aronson, Inc., 1991.

Macy, Howard M. *Laughing Pilgrims: Humor and the Spiritual Journey.* Waynesboro GA: Paternoster Press, 2006.

Martin, Fr. James Martin. *Between Heaven and Mirth.* New York: Harper One, 2011.

McSpadden, Kevin. "You Now Have a Shorter Attention Span than a Goldfish," Time.com, May 14, 2015, time.com/3858309/attention-spans-goldfish/.

Morreall, John. *Comedy, Tragedy and Religion.* Albany: State University of New York Press, 1999.

Moss, Otis, III. *Blue Note Preaching in a Post-Soul World: Finding Hope in an Age of Despair.* Louisville: Westminster John Knox Press, 2015.

Olson, Richard P. *Laughter in a Time of Turmoil: Humor as Spiritual Practice.* Eugene OR: Wipf & Stock, 2012.

Overdorf, Daniel. *One Year to Better Preaching: 52 Exercises to Hone Your Skills.* Grand Rapids: Kregel Publications, 2013.

Rediger, G. Lloyd. *Clergy Killers: Guidance for Pastors and Congregations under Attack.* Louisville KY: Westminster John Knox Press, 1997.

Rosenfield, Stephen. *Mastering Stand-up: The Complete Guide to Becoming a Successful Comedian.* Chicago: Chicago Review Press, 2018.

Samra, Cal. *The Joyful Christ: The Healing Power of Humor.* San Francisco: HarperSanFrancisco, 1977.

Sparks, Susan. *Laugh Your Way to Grace: Reclaiming Humor in the Spiritual Path.* Woodstock VT: Skylight Paths Publishing, 2010.

Taylor, Barbara Brown. *Leaving Church: A Memoir of Faith.* New York: Harper Collins, 2006.

Taylor, Frank A. *How to Preach a Dangerous Sermon.* Nashville: Abingdon, 2018.

Trueblood, Elton. *The Humor of Christ.* New York: Harper & Row, 1964.

Webb, Joseph M. *Comedy and Preaching.* St. Louis MO: Chalice Press, 1998.

———. *Preaching without Notes.* Nashville: Abingdon, 2001.

Wooten, Patty. *Compassionate Laughter: Jest for Your Health.* Salt Lake City UT: Commune-a-Key Publishing, 1996.

ABOUT THE AUTHOR

A trial lawyer turned stand-up comedian and Baptist preacher, Susan Sparks is America's only female comedian with a pulpit. Currently, the senior pastor of the historic Madison Avenue Baptist Church in New York City (and the first woman in its 170-year history), Susan is also a TEDx speaker and a professional comedian appearing with a stand-up rabbi and a Muslim comic in the acclaimed Laugh in Peace Comedy Tour.

A nationally syndicated columnist and author of the award-winning *Laugh Your Way to Grace*, Susan's work with humor and healing has been featured by *O, (The Oprah) Magazine*, the *New York Times*, CNN, and CBS. When not preaching, writing, or speaking, Susan and her husband, Toby, love to fly-fish, ride their Harleys, eat great BBQ, and root for Tarheel basketball and the Green Bay Packers.

Made in the USA
Columbia, SC
19 September 2019